Evolutionary Conservation

Julian Ashbourn

ISBN:1500934410
ISBN-13: 978-1500934415

This book is dedicated to the memory of

Archibald Stansfeld Belaney and Gertrude Bernard

CONTENTS

Chapter	Title	Page No.
1	Introduction	1
2	Evolution Revisited	11
3	The Concept of Conservation	23
4	Evolutionary Conservation	35
5	Introducing the Ecogram	49
6	Introducing the Summary Statement	61
7	Scalability	67
8	Sustainability	79
9	A Practical Methodology	87
10	Tools	97
11	A Framework of Understanding	121
12	Practical Collaboration	129
13	Conclusions	139
14	Appendix 1 - Communications	151
15	Appendix 2 - Animal Biometrics	153
16	Appendix 3 - Grey Owl	161

ACKNOWLEDGMENTS

My very special thanks to all of the friends and associates who gave unselfishly their ongoing encouragement in support of this project, but especially, to my wife Joanna for her enduring understanding and support

1 Introduction

Abstract

This introductory chapter outlines the reality of man's impact upon the natural world and how we have slowly come to understand the need to protect our precious and beautiful planet. It charts the birth of the concept of conservation and some of the key characters who have helped to inform our understanding in this area. Acknowledging the swarming of the human species and the potential damage that we inflict upon natural habitats, we go on to explain the rationale behind the concept and methodology introduced within this book, why we believe this concept to be important and how it might be used in a practical sense. We further explain why we believe it important to ensure that the associated methodology remains simple, elegant and intuitive in use for the benefit of all concerned, introducing the primary tools which support the concept and how they might best be used. It is acknowledged that this chapter sets the scene for the broader discussion undertaken throughout this work.

Introduction

Since early man first set foot upon the Earth, he has interacted with the environment around him and, consequently, has been an agent for change within that environment. Even the early hunter gatherers would have had some impact in this respect, as they roamed across the land, consumed natural resources and did themselves proliferate. When humans started to settle and learned how to cultivate crops, the impact upon natural habitats increased as they cleared areas of land for their own use, thus affecting other species who would otherwise have occupied and made use of the same land. Such activities would have served to polarise different, and sometimes adjacent, habitats together with the species supported by them, thus affecting the interactions and dependencies between these evolving biomes. From those early days onwards, humans have continued to have a significant impact upon the world around them and, as their numbers have increased, the impact has increased accordingly. No other species has affected the environment in which they exist to quite the same degree, impacting both natural habitats and other species as their numbers continued to spiral. Furthermore, as humans systematically extended their reach from one area to another the overall environment, including interactions and dependencies across zones, will have been slowly altered. While we have, no doubt, always been conscious of the effect we were having upon the natural world, attitudes have perhaps changed somewhat as we have come to understand more about natural evolution and the inter-dependencies between both species and environments. In short, we have become increasingly conscious of the need for conserving the precious resources of our living planet. Continued scientific research has served to inform and support the intuitive feeling that we have always had in this context. In recent times, this has particularly highlighted the importance of climate to our own wellbeing and how, to a certain degree at least, climatic change may be influenced by our own actions. However, climatic change, which is of course a natural phenomenon and would be occurring with our without our presence, is simply one of many factors which affect our planet. The greater impact of the human species is undoubtedly that of habitat destruction and all that this entails with respect to species loss and the effects upon both local and broader environments. Ultimately, this affects our own wellbeing and, indeed, our very survival as a species. As we progress into the 21st century, this should be of primary concern for civilisation. Furthermore, the burgeoning and exponential rise in human population renders such a concern imperative as we continue to consume and destroy at an alarming rate. Consequently, it is the right time to consider a mechanism by which we might elevate the concept of conservation to a higher, potentially global level, ensuring that all may participate in a coordinated manner.

The birth of the conservation concept

An appreciation of nature existed even in ancient civilisations, many of which had a better developed respect for animals and the natural world than perhaps we do today. However, it was in the latter half of the 20th century that the concept of conservation, as now popularly understood, gained much ground as people generally became more aware of both the beauty and fragility of the natural world. Commentators such as the late Rachel Carson with her seminal books, The Sea Around Us (1951) and Silent Spring (1962) brought a scientific validity to what many instinctively felt about the way we used the land and oceans and the damage that we are undoubtedly inflicting upon them. Naturalist and broadcaster Sir David Attenborough has, throughout a long and uniquely distinguished career, raised awareness of our natural environments and the species with which we share them. In latter times, he has also drawn attention to the fragility of these environments and the need to protect them. James Lovelock and the late Lynn Margulis reminded us that everything is interconnected upon our living planet and that our actions have consequences and repercussions that we should strive to understand at every level. Others have similarly highlighted the reality of natural processes and the plight of the natural world as human population and consumption continues to increase in an exponential manner. Free thinking amateurs such as Grey Owl (Archie Belaney) brought a colourful awareness of our natural habitats and the threats that they faced via his books and associated lectures in the late 1920s and early 1930s and, since that time, others have likewise raised awareness of our impact upon the natural world.

Consequently, it would be hard to imagine an informed individual on any continent today who does not have an appreciation of the importance of the natural world and the need to protect it. Indeed, even among those less informed and connected, there is typically an instinctive understanding that we should care for our natural environments. This broader understanding is reflected in a large number of initiatives around the world, which may be loosely collected under the banner of conservation. However, the objectives of these initiatives may vary quite widely and may embrace a number of agendas. Some may be seeking a balance between commercial land use and conservation. Some may be attempting to protect endangered species. Some may simply be self promoting academic exercises. Some may be overtly political, and others may reflect a broad spectrum of ideas and objectives. Naturally, each initiative will have an associated local profile and it's own way of realising it's objectives in that context. Different methodologies will be employed and a wide range of views will be expressed accordingly. While each initiative is no doubt well intentioned, there is typically little coordination upon a broader scale and little understanding of related effects beyond the parochial perspective which may, in some instances, negate some of the work undertaken.

This book and the research that it reflects, seeks to address such issues and, in so doing, to introduce a new concept for conservation that is relevant at all scales, from local to regional, from national to international and, ultimately, to global. It is, after all, a global problem that we face. Furthermore, it aims to provide a working methodology with which the underlying concept may be practically realised at every level and which promotes both collaboration and coordination. In addition, the concept and provisions of Evolutionary Conservation may usefully serve to inform national policy and ongoing strategy in a practical and sympathetic manner. Throughout the chapters of this volume, we shall consequently explore many factors which may affect our understanding of conservation and how our various initiatives might better work together for the common good. We are at an important point in our development as a species. Attitudes which we adopt, and decisions which we make at this juncture, will have significant implications for the wellbeing of our planet and, consequently, for future generations of humans. This is a reality that we should fully take into consideration as we plot our course for the future.

Why is Evolutionary Conservation important?

Undoubtedly, the biggest single problem facing us today is the swarming of the human race. Where this situation is leading ultimately is a matter for conjecture. Some would posit that we have already entered a period of mass extinction and that we are, due to our numbers, inviting catastrophic developments which will accelerate this process. Others take a more hopeful view and believe that science will provide us with the means to continue along our evolutionary path, albeit in a much altered manner. Some may hold that numbers will be held in check by spasmodic outbreaks of war, famine or disease. In any event, the population issue is something that we shall probably have little effective control over. After all, no politician is going to advocate a significant reduction in human population within a democratic manifesto. Instead, politicians the world over, prefer to focus upon popular concepts such as climate change and carbon dioxide emissions, not because they care particularly about the fate of the world, but because these are concepts which enable taxation and endless political discussion. Similarly, industry latches on to the same concepts for reasons of overt commercialism. The concept of climate change, real or imagined, is big business and generates significant revenues for many organisations and consultants. It is a sad indictment of the human race that we have allowed a distorted view of science to further an all pervasive culture of greed. Established scientists will readily understand that, actually, carbon dioxide emissions and climate change may, in many ways, be the least of our problems. It is habitat destruction, both terrestrial and within our oceans, that is the pressing problem of the day. And this is an area within which we can exercise a degree of intelligent control.

Instinctively, many people around the world realise that we are destroying natural habitats at an alarming rate and that we ought to be addressing this problem. Consequently, there are many well-meaning initiatives which seek to redress the issue by exercising some sort of control under the broad banner of conservation. Unfortunately, there is relatively little coordination among and between these initiatives which, in turn, lessens their potential impact for the common good. To illustrate this point, imagine a beautiful, sprawling meadow, backing on to a woodland which, together support a variety of species of both flora and fauna. Imagine that we wish to observe and understand the situation in detail and so, we construct a one metre square boundary and place this at a random point within our meadow or woodland. A few metres away, another team does the same and, a few metres from them another team and so on. Within our particular square, we find a selection of species, some of which we don't believe should be there, and so we exercise some control to eliminate them. In another square, the team find that soil quality is rather poor, and so they apply some chemical fertiliser to improve the situation. At yet another square, the team decides that there are too few species, and so they artificially introduce two new species, one of which proves to be invasive and out performs the existing species. A team within the woodland area reasons that there are too many trees blocking the light falling upon their square, and so they remove some of them. All of these may be well meaning initiatives, but none have taken into account the effect of their actions upon either adjacent squares or the broader meadow and woodland. None have understood that their local actions have consequences, some of which may not be observed within their own square, but which may be significant further afield. It is as if we have focused on individual pieces of a large jig saw puzzle, cleaning and repainting each piece to our satisfaction, but with no conception of their position within the whole. This is, in fact, what is happening across our planet with regards to localised conservation initiatives. Similarly, within our oceans, we are aware of specific areas of concern, yet we struggle to place these within a broader context, while we continue to cause wholesale damage in areas which are less conspicuous to the public gaze. Our planet may be likened to a giant and beautiful tapestry which, in many places, is in need of repair. We may choose to undertake these repairs but, in so doing, should step back and understand their effect upon the broader picture that the tapestry depicts. However, unlike a tapestry, our planet is a dynamic, living entity. Therefore, any changes we make have a much broader effect than simply visible alteration. Indeed, such changes will affect the entire natural dynamic which, itself, incorporates mechanisms for reaction and compensation. It is a complex entity which requires a deep understanding if we are to interact with it in a sympathetic and intelligent manner.

The first parameter we must embrace is one of observation and classification. We must understand exactly what we are dealing with at every level, from local, through regional and national, to international and global. Realising this understanding in a common language is one of the tenets of Evolutionary Conservation. Furthermore, such an understanding must be aligned with the concept of time and change, and in a manner which allows for a degree of prediction and correlation across boundaries. The mechanism used to articulate this understanding must also be intuitive and easily used at every level, regardless of language or scientific discipline. It must be simple enough for a child to understand, yet powerful enough to form the basis of a global framework of scientific understanding. Evolutionary Conservation answers this challenge with a simple device called an ecogram. We shall cover the use of the ecogram, together with other associated tools, elsewhere in this volume. Suffice it to say, that we need such a mechanism in order to broaden the horizon of our understanding of conservation and how we might practice our good intentions upon a wider, more sympathetic level for the benefit of the common good. This is the primary goal of the concept of Evolutionary Conservation.

Who can use Evolutionary Conservation?

Sometimes, within the field of scientific endeavour, we develop concepts and mechanisms which, while undoubtedly useful, require such an in depth understanding of the particular discipline involved, that many remain unable to use them effectively. Even worse, they may, in their attempts to grapple with them, use them incorrectly, thus producing erroneous results of questionable value. This situation has been further complicated in recent years with the inexorable rise of Information Technology. These days, scientists must also, it seems, be computer programmers. However, the vagaries of computer operating systems and development languages conspire to overlay their own inconsistencies upon the situation. The result is often computer models which behave in an unpredictable manner, yielding inferences in which we may not entertain an appropriate degree of confidence. A good example may be found within the plethora of climate modelling and prediction tools currently available, in which, the more granular the query, the more variable the output. At a lower level of abstraction, the ability to understand whether such mechanisms and tools are producing accurate outputs will be constrained to a relatively small group of individuals. Other users may take the outputs at face value. Worse, important decisions may be made based on such outputs and the inferences that are made from them. This is an unsatisfactory state of affairs and one which, ideally, should have no place in science. And yet, this is often the reality within major initiatives. Of course, some tools may be perfectly good, but the casual operators ability to quantify them as such may be constrained by their understanding of exactly how the tools are operating at the lower level. This information will exist in the heads of a relatively few individuals.

An objective of Evolutionary Conservation is therefore that anyone should be able to use the simple mechanism provided, and to readily understand it. Young students at school should be able to grasp it immediately, as should undergraduates whose primary discipline lies elsewhere. It should also be readily, and intuitively understood by lay people in any country of the world. In this respect, politicians and decision makers may easily grasp the concept and understand why it is important from the broader, global perspective. In this context, Evolutionary Conservation holds the potential to support an international framework of understanding (FOU) which may serve in an advisory capacity for the benefit of related initiatives at every level. Furthermore, this framework of understanding will be, in itself, dynamic and will, over the years evolve an increasingly complete picture of global conservation and the direction in which it should be headed for the common good. In addition, the information which supports this understanding may be made readily available to all concerned and maintained accordingly. Any associated software tools will reflect this simplicity of approach and will remain intuitive and easily used for all who need access to them. All of this, and more, may be realised via the concept of Evolutionary Conservation and the simple methodology that it introduces. It is a methodology which, like all good things in science, is simple, intuitive and practically operable. It is also extendible, should it prove necessary to develop it further.

How may the methodology be used?

The underlying principle of Evolutionary Conservation is one of observation. The ecogram, and it's associated classifications, introduces a reliable and consistent method of quantifying natural habitats at every level. A single ecogram is useful in itself as a statement in time of a particular environment and its ecosystem, however small. A collection of ecograms, perhaps for a regional area, provides a wealth of additional detail, together with an appreciation of the dynamics involved. This may be articulated within the associated summary statements and provides a sound basis for tailoring individual initiatives in alignment with the broader regional picture. As we extrapolate the concept to a national level, the understanding becomes ever deeper as new trends and situations are identified. More pertinent advice may now be proffered to individual initiatives. This reality is a product of the myriad of dependencies and interactions which exist within our natural world and which will be exposed by systematic observation. The broader we cast the geographic net, the greater the depth and number of these interactions, many of which would simply not be discernible at the local, or even regional level. This is the whole point of Evolutionary Conservation: to be able to incrementally develop our understanding of the broader, global picture and how these interactions and dependencies work. This understanding, in turn, must be based upon observation and not theory or supposition. Ecograms may be produced at every level and brought together at increasing levels of extrapolation in order to document our understanding. At each of the higher levels, our understanding is enriched until, at the global level, we are able to develop a realistic appreciation of the current status of our planet and precisely how our conservation efforts should be informed and coordinated for the common good. It may take a while to reach this ideal. However, the benefits of practising Evolutionary Conservation may be realised immediately at local and regional levels, with a minimum of explanation and training. Databases and other utilities will be freely provided in this respect.

The first step along this path will be to take ecogram templates out into the field and to embark upon a systematic documentation of discernible environmental areas. These may be accurately described by latitude and longitude references and given a unique identifier according to a common naming convention. After gathering current information, the ecogram may be supplemented by prior information from known records and other sources and entered into the local database. Predictive inferences may then be made, together with conclusions as to areas of concern. In such a manner, a revealing and comprehensive picture of a particular environment may be evolved and documented in a simple, universal manner. More detailed information will be provided elsewhere in this volume as to the proper use of ecograms and the common classifications that underpin their use. As we extrapolate this approach across local areas, we automatically develop an in depth regional understanding which is itself enriched over successive seasons of operation. These regional perspectives, in turn, automatically generate a comprehensive national perspective which may additionally be used to inform national environmental policy. For the first time, we shall have a comprehensive and detailed understanding of the national environment in its entirety, from which intelligent and environmentally sympathetic inferences may be made. When we extrapolate the concept across national boundaries, a further level of understanding is realised, providing us with a rich perspective, not only of the current situation and how it may be developing, but of how actions in one area may cause reactions in another, or may otherwise have implications for the wellbeing of wildlife and species in general. This level of understanding, in turn, develops into a solid body of informed expertise from which intelligent appraisals and recommendations may be made within an international framework of understanding. This would surely be a most desirable situation at this juncture. Furthermore, it is a situation that is easily within our grasp. This book outlines a practical methodology, together with a workable process by which it may be established and maintained into the future, for the common good of all who care for our beautiful planet and the wonder of life supported upon it.

Summary

This chapter started with an introduction to the concept of conservation, how it has evolved and why it is needed, before moving on to introduce the concept of Evolutionary Conservation in broad terms. It has explained how our current approach to conservation, while well intentioned, does not fully take into account the broader global perspective, with all its complex interactions and dependencies, and has stressed the need for a better coordination of effort, under an international framework of understanding, itself a product of the Evolutionary Conservation initiative. The new ecogram mechanism has been introduced, and has been described as an intuitive and easily used methodology which underpins the Evolutionary Conservation concept. The practical usage of the ecogram has been similarly described, stressing the various layers at which it may be used and how an increasingly broad and detailed perspective may be developed as a result. The potential benefits of such an approach may be easily comprehended.

This chapter has, in many ways, set the scene for a broader discussion around contemporary conservation and it's applicability to the future of our living planet. Within this broad scope, there exist many factors which may be considered, none more pertinent than the relationships, interactions and dependencies, among and between our natural environments and the species that they support. This interconnectivity is the key to natural evolution upon our planet and is consequently a key factor with regard to the future wellbeing of all species, including the human species. Understanding this interconnectivity lies at the heart of Evolutionary Conservation as a concept. It provides us with a portfolio of ideas and mechanisms with which to realise this understanding in an intuitive manner, across boundaries of both geography and culture, and in support of the common good. The manner in which the various mechanisms for this realisation may be used, will be further discussed throughout the pages of this volume.

2. Evolution Revisited

Abstract

In this chapter, we acknowledge the miracle of life and how early man might have mused over the wonder that surrounded him within the rich tapestry of flora and fauna upon our beautiful planet. We continue to the struggle to understand the organisation and evolution of species within the sphere of early scientific and religious belief and the breakthrough which came with Charles Darwin, while acknowledging others who helped develop our understanding as careful observation supplanted assumption and superstition. Moving forwards, we discuss the development of our understanding of DNA and the genetic mechanism and how this helped to consolidate our broader understanding. We conclude with a reflection upon our journey of discovery along the road to our understanding of evolution and an acknowledgement of the importance of this evolutionary understanding to our aspirations around conservation.

Introduction

We exist upon a living planet. Everywhere around us we may observe the miracle of life in the abundance of flora and fauna which natural processes have provided, fuelled by a combination of the Earth's radioactive core and our juxtaposition within the solar system. There further exists a myriad of layers upon which this orchestration of life takes place, each with their own dynamic and each interlocking and reacting with the other within this complex and beautiful tapestry of life on Earth. The dynamic extends beyond the biological, to the very heart of the planet and the processes which move continents and create mountains within their longer term tectonic ballet. Indeed, our entire planet exists within a constant state of change. Evolution is the key to almost everything that we understand about life on Earth, from the changing shape of continents to the smallest biological organism. It lies at the heart of every process and at the juncture of every interaction and dependency within our complex living planet. It is fitting therefore, that we consider the natural evolutionary processes when we attempt to protect or conserve our natural habitats and the species that they support. It is posited that conservation, without an understanding of evolution, represents a concept unnecessarily constrained by it's own definition. We cannot lock things in time, that is simply not how nature operates. There is a greater, more wondrous and more beautiful dynamic which we must strive to understand and with which we should work in sympathy. Consequently, in this chapter, we shall revisit our understanding of evolution, at least at a high level, in order to make this connection.

In the beginning

Man has probably always wondered about the mechanisms of the natural world. The earliest of our ancestors could not have failed to be moved by the beauty of a tree, the power of the oceans, or the magnificence of the night sky. Ancient civilisations certainly expended a good deal of time and effort in understanding the progress of the celestial bodies and, no doubt, strived to understand the processes and structure of the natural world around them and what lay beyond our own planet. It was perhaps predictable that what could not be readily explained from a purely logical perspective, would be entwined with religious doctrines of one sort or another which, in part due to the power base associated with them, would endure for some considerable time. Indeed, even today, the creationist theories hold sway in many areas, in spite of considerable evidence which is incompatible with such a notion, while conversely, there remain realities which science itself has no explanation for. Consequently, throughout history, those far sighted individuals who sought rational explanation for the wonder of nature which they observed in every quarter, often found acceptance of their ideas very difficult, in some cases to the point of being persecuted for daring to think outside of the strict constraints of the particular religious doctrine under whose jurisdiction they happened to fall. However, this situation would slowly change and, as the age of enlightenment drew on from around the middle of the 17th century, philosophers and others started to question the older doctrines and enquire increasingly into the nature of things and the reasons for our existence. Indeed, one might posit that even before this time we were on the path of understanding evolution as we learned more about the human anatomy via dissection. Across Europe, in universities such as Paris, Bologna, Padua and elsewhere, anatomy was being taught from the medical perspective and advances were being made as to our understanding of the human body and how it functioned. Assumptions gave way to knowledge based upon careful observation and meticulous documentation.

What we might now call scientific reasoning was becoming widespread across various disciplines from medicine to astronomy, replacing a previous reliance upon tradition and superstition.

With respect to our understanding of evolution, things were also changing. For a while, there was a fascination with the idea of recapitulation, a veritable 'ladder of life' wherein species took their place upon the ladder in accordance with a strict organisation, with humans, naturally, at the top. There existed several variations on this theme while, in the background, the science of palaeontology was slowly gaining ground. It was eventually recognised, after much debate, that fossils reflected living organisms from previous times and that this provided us with a record of how life had evolved on Earth, although their placement initially left many questions unanswered. It was also becoming clear that our living planet was considerably older than had previously been supposed. Such notions caused many to think again about life on Earth and the processes by which it evolved. Among them was Jean Baptiste Pierre Antoine de Monet, Chevalier de Lamarck. In 1809, Lamarck published his Philosphie Zoologique in which he proposed his own theory of evolution. In this, he acknowledged that life is not fixed, but instead moves along a developmental continuum. As a result of this process occurring over an extended time period, many species were occupying the Earth simultaneously, although the point of their inception would be scattered along this time line. The origin of species was a concept that Lamarck struggled with. He proposed that species were created by a spontaneous generation from non-living matter and that they slowly evolved from this point, moving up the evolutionary ladder as they developed into increasingly complex organisms. At the top of this imaginary ladder of species, was man himself. Incremental development was, according to Lamarck's theory, enabled by a 'nervous fluid' within each species, which interacted with the physical reality of life, flowing into the most used appendages and developing them accordingly. Thus, when a giraffe repeatedly reached for higher leaves upon a tree, the neck would receive an additional input of nervous fluid and would start to develop in sympathy with the functional requirement, becoming longer and more articulate. Such an alteration in a single specimen, was passed down and inherited by the next generation, and so on, creating incremental development over time. While Lamarck's view of evolution was undoubtedly flawed, we are indebted to him for at least providing a unified theory of evolution which was properly considered and documented. His contemporaries may have chosen to agree or disagree with his philosophy, but Lamarck was forthright enough to publish his theories at a time when there would have been a somewhat negative response to any such suggestions from those who supported the creationist view. As it turned out, Lamarck's ideas were not particularly well received within his own life time. Yet he remains an important figure within the history of evolutionary thinking.

Observation displaces assumption

Meanwhile, observations in other areas were slowly changing our view of the world. Geologists started to understand that the clearly discernible layers that they observed in rock formations actually represented different time periods, and that these periods probably extended back some considerable time. It was also becoming clear that the very fabric of our terrestrial world was not static, but moved around over extended periods of time. This explained why fossils from marine organisms were occasionally found on mountain sides. Clearly, there was a broader evolution to consider: that of the planet itself. However, placing the observable layers into any kind of logical order and assigning dates to them was problematic. Ironically, progress in this area was made, not by a philosopher, or even an established geologist, but by an unknown canal surveyor by the name of William Smith. It was Smith who, while supervising the digging of the Somerset canal in England, started to notice an order in the stratigraphy of the rocks as they cut through them. In particular, fossils appeared in a discernible sequence from the lower layers toward those uppermost in the hierarchy. Furthermore, as he travelled increasingly around England, he observed precisely the same patterns appearing at other sites. Smith realised that the fossils he was observing had been living in different time periods, as indicated by the layers of rock that had built up, one upon the other. In the early 1800's Smith started to meticulously create a geological map of England based upon his observations. It took him sixteen years to complete and, when finally published, was not initially well received by the established geologists of the day. It was much later, in 1831, when the value of his work was finally acknowledged and he was awarded the prestigious Wollaston medal by the Geological Society in London. Others then followed Smith's example and observations elsewhere lead to the creation of additional geological maps. At around the same time, geologist Charles Lyell began to consider the time periods involved in these episodes, and concluded that the Earth evolved over a considerable time via uniform processes, rather than as a result of periodic catastrophic events as was widely held at that time.

Consequently, our view of the Earth and it's history, including that of the many species who occupied it, began to change.

From a species evolutionary perspective, one factor that scientists had been struggling with was the concept of heredity and how observable characteristics were passed down from one generation to the next. While Darwin and others were pondering such matters, far away in a monastery in what is now the Czech Republic, Gregor Mendel was experimenting with pea plants. Mendel, who had come from an agricultural background, was also fascinated by the manner in which traits in plants were inherited from one generation to another. He undertook a meticulous study of peas, cross breeding them in a controlled manner and noting modification among a specific set of observable traits. Mendel bred many thousands of pea plants and noticed that, very often, the immediate hybrids from one paring did not exhibit the expected traits, such as coarseness of texture for example, and yet this trait would reappear in the next generation. It was as if the trait had been there all along but, for some reason, was not being expressed. With our current understanding of genetics, we understand this as dominant or recessive genes according to the state of the associated alleles. However, in Mendel's time there was no such understanding and, sadly, his work passed mostly unrecognised during his lifetime and Mendel resumed his monastic duties. It wasn't until fifteen years after his death that other scientists understood the significance of his work in relation to the understanding inheritance.

A breakthrough

And so, further progress was being made in our understanding of evolution. As often happens in the field of scientific endeavour, while many are pondering a set of associated problems, one individual will suddenly make a leap forwards and piece together a scenario which takes our thinking forward to the next level. Within the sphere of evolution, it was of course Charles Darwin. The nucleus of his thinking had been formed back in the days of his voyage on the Beagle and the observations he made around species at that time, especially those on the Galapagos islands in 1835. Yet he continued with his research for many years, noting how pigeon breeders selectively bred birds in order to produce certain traits and how this process fitted with his own observations around natural selection. It was with the publication of 'On the Origins of Species' in 1859 that Darwin's work really came together and made an enormous impact, not only within the scientific world, but within society as a whole. In particular, the idea of descent from a common ancestor did not fit comfortably with those who favoured the creationist theory. Darwin, who had himself been a religious man, was well aware that this would be the case, and it was one of the reasons why he delayed the publication of his work for so long. In the intermediate years, he had corresponded with many on the subject, including Alfred Russel Wallace, who had been undertaking research of a similar kind in the South Americas. When Wallace sent Darwin his notes in 1858, asking for his opinion as to their suitability for publication, it was with great surprise that Darwin realised that Wallace had independently come to very similar conclusions as his own. It was decided that both Darwin's and Wallace's theories would be presented at a meeting of the Linnaean Society in London and this was arranged by Charles Lyell and Joseph Hooker. Curiously, the joint theories, when presented, did not meet with anything but casual interest and it seems that the society members failed to grasp the significance of this work. However, the general public had no such difficulty and 'On the Origins of Species' quickly became a best seller. Our understanding of evolution had taken a giant step forwards. Darwin continued with his work and, some would hold, took on far too much, which probably contributed to his continuous bouts of ill health in later years. He looked into many areas, including geology, the effect that earth worms had on soil formation and, of course, published his other hugely influential work, 'The Descent of Man'. He died in April 1882 and was buried in Westminster Abbey.

Darwin certainly set other scientists thinking about evolution in new ways. However, the concept of natural selection was something that many continued to struggle with, years after the publication of 'On the Origins of Species'. To some, it seemed logical that there must be some purpose to the direction of evolution and that the notion of randomness and chance did not fit comfortably with this. It was much later, in the 1920s, when our understanding of genetics was developing, that the idea was revisited in the light of our advanced knowledge. The work undertaken by scientists such as Ronald Fisher, JBS Haldane and Sewall Wright served to validate Darwin's concept of natural selection by showing how small changes could occur via genetic mutations and that, if these changes proved beneficial, they would be reproduced down the hereditary chain. Furthermore, Fisher, Haldane and Wright built mathematical models to show how evolution and natural selection could work via incremental small changes. Their approach, together with that of others working in this area, became known as Population Genetics and acknowledged that alleles at a given locus within the genetic strand could be effectively switched in a seemingly random manner, causing changes to be reflected throughout a given population. This and other work would be subsumed into what became known as the Modern Synthesis. A modern synthesis of evolution.

Understanding DNA

However, observing such mechanisms in action at the lower, genetic level was fraught with difficulty, because nobody really understood what the genetic structure actually looked like. It was therefore impossible to compare two different states at this level, even if we could observe phenotypic changes taking place. Consequently, there was something of a race to find the molecular architecture or structure of what we now call DNA. Many leading scientists around the world were engaged in research to discover this structure. It was a far from straightforward task to detect these molecules of DNA as they could only be observed under a complicated x-ray process whereby beams were deflected from the associated atoms and formed an observable pattern on film. One scientist who became expert in this area was Rosalind Franklin. She happened to be working at Cambridge where two other scientists, named James Watson and Francis Crick were also puzzling over the structure of DNA. Partly inspired by the work of Franklin and Maurice Wilkins, whose department she operated within, they decided to build a physical model of the DNA structure in order to further develop their ideas. As they worked on their model, it assumed the form of a twisted ladder or double helix (a form corroborated by one of Franklin's images), with the two runners of the ladder representing phosphates and sugars and the rungs representing pairs of organic compounds or bases. Others were of course working on ideas and models of their own, including the renowned scientist Linus Pauling over in California. Something of a race was developing to solve the DNA puzzle. But Watson and Crick were on the right path and persevered with their model, from which they would eventually determine the mechanism of DNA as we understand it today. After a good deal of discussion and refinement, Watson and Crick had finally solved the puzzle, a distinction which was to later win them the Nobel Prize.

From this significant step forward, scientists could determine what was actually happening at a genetic level. The accepted thinking became that a specific gene, at a particular locus upon the genome, consisted of a set of base pairs, as introns and exons defined by a start and stop codon. This single strand was transposed, via removal of the introns to messenger RNA, passed to protein building ribosomes which, in turn assembled a set of amino acids according to the genetic code in order to form a new protein. Mutations at the base pair level could therefore cause variations further on in the process, resulting in the random changes which lie at the heart of natural selection. In this manner, a mutation which happened to confer a practical advantage to the organism in question, might be readily replicated by successful breeding throughout a population. We now had a mechanism with which to support the concept of natural selection and adaptation. However, while we have made huge strides in our understanding of genetics, there remain some peculiarities which test this understanding. For example, in addition to the mutations referred to, entire portions of the genome may be replicated in a seemingly random manner. Furthermore, there may be significant regions which appear to be effectively non-coding. There may also be transcription errors which will affect the outcome. All of these variations are likely within the scope of a particular organism. Indeed, the process of cell replication via the genetic mechanism clearly has an inherent flexibility which allows for evolutionary change, for better or for worse. Opinions may differ as to just how random these processes are. Is it really all down to chance mutations? The miracle of life is complex. As are many of the phenotypic expressions, some of which have an extraordinary symmetrical beauty which itself challenges the concept of randomness. Perhaps our understanding is in its infancy after all. Nevertheless, such an understanding of the mechanisms and actuality of evolution must surely be incorporated into our aspirations towards the ongoing care of our world.

Conclusions

Our journey along the path of evolutionary understanding has been most fascinating. It has shown to us, in particular, the dynamic composition of the natural world and how this inherent flexibility allows for evolutionary change. However, it is a journey which is surely not over yet. There remain factors for which we have no easy answer and complexities which remain tantalisingly out of our reach. Perhaps we shall continue along this path of discovery and unravel some of these complexities. What we do know is that everything around us is subject to evolutionary change. Furthermore, the rate of change is itself dynamic and varies considerably across organisms. Even the very fabric of our tangible world, the geosphere, is itself a dynamic entity, albeit working to different time scales. This rich dynamic tapestry of our beautiful living planet is further enhanced by the complex web of interactions and dependencies which exist within and between species and habitats at every level. One might compare this mechanism of interactions and dependencies with the genetic mechanism itself. Both are wondrous mechanisms of which we have a certain level of understanding, and yet which exhibit a certain randomness and inherent beauty which challenges that very understanding. This dynamic tapestry may be visualised as a rich, colourful kaleidoscope of life which is constantly changing before our eyes. This is the nature of evolution.

In modern times, we have come to understand the fundamentals of genetics and, in so doing, have almost completed a puzzle which started when man first questioned his own existence and the wonder of life around him, and which reached a high point with Darwin and Wallace. With this foundation of understanding to build upon, we have been able to delve ever deeper into the mysteries of life, occasionally developing new theories, such as the concept of symbioses as described by the late Lynn Margulis. It was accepted that new organisms always sprang from existing organisms according to the principles of a single common ancestor and an ever expanding tree of life. Margulis argued however that there may well have been symbiotic events which effectively combined elements from separate organisms in order to produce a completely new example. In 1970, she published her ideas in the paper entitled 'The Origin of Eukaryotic Cells'. Later it was shown that the DNA inside chloroplasts within plant cells, was different from the DNA within the nucleus, thus supporting the view that Margulis had been proposing since the early 1960s. This example demonstrates that our knowledge remains incomplete and that there is always scope to expand upon what we know, or what we think we know.

Within the context of this particular volume, the fundamental point to acknowledge is that the evolution of our planet and the life that it supports is orchestrated via a mechanism of constant change. We now understand a good deal about how that mechanism works, although our knowledge remains incomplete in many areas. One of the objectives of Evolutionary Conservation as proposed within this work, is to provide a methodology which will enable us to study and document our world in a uniform manner, noting how evolutionary change has worked in the past and trying to understand how it might work in the future. This methodology will encourage an enhanced understanding of interactions and dependencies, of cause and effect, and will therefore enable us to make better informed decisions with respect to our various conservation initiatives, whatever their scale, and whoever is undertaking them. This enhanced understanding is underpinned by our appreciation of the evolutionary model, an understanding which has been painstakingly developed over many years of research and observation. Looking back over this period, one wonders what we shall learn in the next fifty years or so? Will our journey along this road help us to really understand and protect our fragile world? Shall we learn fast enough for this to be a reality? Will science supplant politics and commercialism with respect to key decisions? These are just some of the questions that arise as the human race continues to proliferate and change the environment in which we live. Ever since early man first looked at the world around him and questioned his own existence, we have been learning about the natural world and the miracle of life upon our beautiful planet. Is our knowledge now sufficiently secure to be able to make intelligent decisions about our own future on Earth? For we are intimately entwined with the natural world and its destiny. We may still have a long way to go along our road of evolutionary understanding, and yet we do have a certain level of knowledge. It is surely time for us to start using that knowledge wisely. It is hoped that the Evolutionary Conservation model, as described in this volume, may help us to apply our knowledge in a practical manner.

Summary

This chapter has focused upon evolution and how we have come to our current understanding of evolutionary concepts and associated mechanisms. It has taken a long time for us to understand the mechanics of evolution, such as we do, with many false starts along the way. Even following the ground breaking work of Charles Darwin, we struggled to find how natural selection worked in practice and from a biological perspective, even though we could readily observe the reality of the process. Our new understanding of genetics filled a gap in the framework of knowledge that Darwin, Wallace and others had constructed and we now have a more comprehensive view of the evolutionary model, although our understanding remains incomplete in some respects. Furthermore, future discoveries may serve to enlighten our understanding of evolution, as science rarely stands still.

What we have come to understand however is that our beautiful, living planet is a dynamic entity within which there are complex relationships, interactions and dependencies, which we must strive to comprehend if we are to protect our natural world for the benefit of future generations, as well as for the other species with whom we share our planet and without whom our lives would have less meaning. The ongoing development of this understanding, in a manner which supports the concept of conservation, is the focus of this work, within which a practical methodology will be defined and offered for this purpose. The reality of evolution cannot be separated from our natural world and its development. It follows that an evolutionary understanding must be woven into our concept of conservation in a manner which allows for a more coordinated and sympathetic approach to be taken to individual initiatives. This requirement is one of the tenets of Evolutionary Conservation and has driven the development of the Evolutionary Conservation methodology. This methodology will be described and explored in some detail within subsequent chapters.

3. The Concept of Conservation

Abstract

In this chapter, we start with a brief coverage of the origins of conservation and the segregation of land for special purposes. We consider how, throughout civilisation, the appreciation of the natural world has been reflected in the arts and, eventually, within the sciences, and the formation of the national parks. We move on to consider the definition of conservation as popularly understood and how political and commercial interests can influence this perspective. We discuss the need for a purer, more universally accepted definition, together with working methodologies in order to support the same. We look at conservation in practice and explore potential deficiencies in our approach and how the adoption of too parochial a view may lead to inadequacies upon the broader scale. Lastly, we consider the implications of our current approach and provide some examples to illustrate why we might usefully modify our thinking and take a broader perspective.

Introduction

It may be argued that conservation started in the middle ages with the English kings wishing to segregate portions of land for hunting purposes. These royal hunting grounds were protected from exploitation by local residents in order to ensure the presence of plentiful game for the royal hunting parties. Consequently, several areas of land were effectively reserved for such purposes. An interesting example may be seen today in the New Forest area of Hampshire, a protected area created by William the Conqueror in 1079. At that time there was a very strong legal underpinning to the concept of such protected land, which was not well received by the general populace. This situation was further exacerbated by the punitive penalties for anyone found stealing or killing the game which, at some points in time included the death penalty. Ironically, the son of William the Conqueror, William II, or William Rufus as he has become popularly known, died in this very forest while hunting deer in the year 1100. William II had been particularly strict with respect to his governance of the land and his passing was not mourned by the local population. Eventually. the laws were relaxed and commoners were granted the right to graze their own livestock on this land, a practice which continues to this day and which, to some degree, accounts for the currently perceived constitution of the New Forest.

Segregating areas of land for reasons other than what we would now call conservation also happened elsewhere, including in the Americas, where the indigenous peoples were granted parcels of land for their own use. The politics of such practices may be argued from various perspectives, but the legacy lives on. The term 'reservation' has been largely replaced by the term 'community' and, in Canada for example, some of these communities exist within areas of distinctive natural beauty. In Saskatchewan, under treaty No.6, such an area was created in 1876 by negotiation with Governor Alexander Morris and the Woodlands and Plains Cree Indians. Modifications to this treaty ensured that, by 1897, this area stretched over 36,000 acres and, in 1948, was divided between the Montreal Lake Reserve and the Little Red River Reserve. Today, this area remains ecologically important, as acknowledged by the First Nations communities who reside there. Elsewhere in the world, we may find other examples of land segregation and effective protection for reasons other than what we would now call conservation.

However, segregating portions of land for the purposes of cultivation and, in many cases, for aesthetic reasons, is a practice which, almost certainly, goes back to ancient civilisations. Indeed, the very notion of civilisation is concerned with human beings creating a sense of permanence by imprinting their ideas upon the world around them, whether in the form of great monuments, of art or of simply modifying the land for their particular use. Much of this would of course be entwined with agriculture and, in some cases, even religious belief, as would be the relationship between humans and the rest of the animal kingdom. The ancient Egyptians, for example, had a healthy respect for animals, as is evident from their own, beautiful mythology. The North American and Canadian Indians likewise had a positive relationship with the land and their fellow creatures. While it may be argued that our treatment of animals and the land throughout some of those periods was less than sympathetic, there was at least a realisation of the importance of the natural world and the need to treat it with respect. From a purely practical point of view, we accepted the need to work in close harmony with nature and, furthermore, such an understanding existed, almost instinctively, within every strata of society. Perhaps an element of this almost universal thread found its way through to the middle ages and the idea of formally segregating and protecting parcels of land.

In parallel with such developments, a growing awareness of the beauty of the natural world was beginning to be reflected in the arts. Poets, writers and painters all turned their attention to this theme. In England, artists such as Constable and Turner depicted natural landscapes for their own sake rather than simply as backdrops for human activity. In the Americas also, early settlers started to appreciate the beauty and wonder of the magnificent land that they now called home, and this realisation was similarly reflected in the arts. In 1872, the creation of the Yellowstone National Park represented a milestone in the appreciation of nature, even if there was an overtly commercial bias to the undertaking. Shortly afterwards in 1883, the area that is now known as Banff National Park was established following the discovery of natural hot springs by railway workers pushing towards the Pacific coast. There followed a programme of National Parks creation in Canada which, from the very beginning, had a strong bias towards conservation and protection of the land for the common good. This heritage is reflected today in the good work undertaken by Parks Canada and their concept of ecological integrity. In the late 1940s, the British presence in Africa, conscious of the fragility of the natural environment and its species which they had come to appreciate, established large wildlife preserves which also served to raise awareness of the plight of our natural world. The sum of such activities ensured that the concept of conservation had effectively been sown in the international consciousness, albeit at a general level. It was becoming clear that, if we don't look after our precious and beautiful world, we would start to loose both the natural habitats and the species which they support. Unfortunately, in parallel with this philosophy, exists the realisation of exploitation and commercial gain via the destruction of that same natural world which has been revered since the birth of civilisation itself. In modern times, we have a new strain of barbarism, motivated by greed and practised at every level, even when protestations are made to the contrary by a plethora of official bodies, committees, organisations and societies. It is against this barbarism that the modern conservationist must be prepared to stand and, if need be, fight. It is a struggle of a scale never before experienced upon Earth. It is, indeed, a struggle for civilisation, as no collection of humans worthy of that appellation would ever tolerate the wide scale destruction of natural habitats and species which we are currently witnessing.

Defining conservation

Today, the concept of conservation is well established internationally, with a brace of regional initiatives, complemented by a plethora of conferences and various associations and organisations all affirming the need to protect our planet and its environs. In addition, the topic has become both political and commercial, with the former advocates seeking to gain political advantage and the latter seeking to gain commercial advantage by association with the broader concept of conservation. Such a development would not necessarily be a bad thing if it meant an increased flow of practical support and funding for intelligently conceived initiatives. Unfortunately, this is not always the case, although there is no reason why it should not be so. Consequently, the public perception of conservation is distorted slightly by the visible face of such activities. This in turn may lead to the execution of initiatives which, while well intentioned, may be constrained by the politically oriented supply chain. The academic position may similarly be influenced by funding and a degree of political correctness, thus affecting the type and location of associated research. One might argue that any conservation initiative must be a good thing, regardless of its origins or management. However, this may not necessarily be the case, at least not in the longer term. It is possible that a localised initiative actually weakens the potential for a broader, regional understanding. Habitats have both a spatial and temporal context which must be understood if we are to further understand species diversity and conservation on a broader scale. In addition, it is quite possible that well meaning initiatives serve to shift the perceived problem elsewhere or even create new pockets of exploitation and habitat destruction. This is unfortunate as there are a large number of such well intentioned activities often orchestrated by enthusiastic and dedicated individuals who are passionate about the need to protect our natural habitats and the species which they support. However, many of these individual initiatives would benefit from a stronger, more unified support at the national level. Consequently, the politics of conservation needs to be much better informed and better able to serve in a practical manner in support of individual initiatives. The Evolutionary Conservation mechanism provides for this requirement.

Perhaps we need to return to a fundamental definition of conservation which may apply across boundaries of both geography, culture and politics and remain operable for the common good, no matter where it is applied. This will not be easy due to the different pressures and situations that occur regionally. For example, in some areas, the balance between land use for commercial development and conservation will take on a different meaning according to historic activities and the available alternative means of support for local communities. In other areas, the balance will be much clearer, although this does not necessarily mean that conservation will triumph over commercial exploitation. Indeed, the opposite is the norm. Government surely has an important part to play in this respect as, through legislation and the enforcement of legislation, it may ensure that, at least within the confines of its own borders, natural habitats and the species which they support may be protected. In some countries, this approach is evident within the management of national parks, but falls down outside of these protected areas. In other countries, it doesn't even get that far. Often, commercial considerations readily take precedence and these are often emphasised by the stance of those benefiting from them, usually asserting that no other course is possible. It is in such situations that well informed government should take the lead and prioritise accordingly. We need to take the longer term view and ensure that our conservation efforts are both practical and sustainable. The development of such a view may be supported by well orchestrated academic research, founded upon solid scientific principles and underpinned by the wealth of our existing knowledge. The starting point is a common definition of our objectives for the common good. In this respect, the time has surely come for us to think from a global perspective, and to try our best to understand the complex web of relationships and dependencies which underpin our natural world. Elsewhere in this volume we shall consider a mechanism with which such an understanding may be developed, communicated and practically supported. It is the mechanism of Evolutionary Conservation.

Conservation in practice

We instinctively feel that we must care for and protect our beautiful planet. From an evolutionary perspective, it may transpire that we are but temporary caretakers, in which case, it is surely all the more important that we strive to understand, respect and preserve the natural processes which have been in operation for many, many millions of years. The burgeoning weight of humanity is having a very significant impact upon this natural world. We cannot help that. Our very numbers ensure that this will be the case and, in any event, we are an integral component of that natural world. However, we are uniquely blessed with an advanced understanding of the world and its mechanisms, and this places us in an interesting position.

More than any other species, we are coming to understand the consequences of our own activities within a world of finite natural resources, and equally cognisant of our duty of care towards this world. This modern, scientifically informed awareness has been developing systematically for several decades now. We know what we should be doing in order to protect our natural habitats and yet, the wholesale alteration and destruction of them continues while, in parallel, we have established more conservation organisations and associated initiatives than we can shake a stick at. Some of these are effective, at least upon their defined scale. Some of them less so. Some are undeniably politically inspired. Some become bottomless pits for funding and some make for good media material, while some are simply academic exercises. Among this cornucopia of mixed intentions, we hope that at least some of these initiatives will serve to protect our natural habitats and the species within them. Certainly, there have been some notable and praiseworthy efforts in this direction. But the question remains; are we really doing enough to protect our world, given the degree of knowledge that we now posses? How is it that, with all these various groups and organisations we still have a massive and enduring problem? Where does conservation really sit among the list of national and international priorities? Forget the politics and ballyhoo. We have arrived at a juncture where we need to be thinking very seriously about what is realisable with respect to the protection of our beautiful planet and how best to execute our plans. It may transpire that time is not on our side and the sooner we start to think globally, the better for all concerned. This thinking must start with common definitions, common priorities and a willingness to coordinate our efforts for the benefit of the common good.

Deficiencies in our approach

As previously indicated, there are many well intentioned initiatives, often supported by volunteers, which achieve a degree of success within the bounds of their self defined scope. However, it is this very concept of scope with which we struggle. For example, when the scope is narrowly defined, perhaps in relation to the protection of a single species, it is easy to inadvertently cause further problems. This has often been the case when non-indigenous species have been introduced and have upset the natural balance within a given habitat. Similarly, if the scope is narrowly defined from a spatial perspective, it is easy to cause a negative impact to adjacent territories and their species, if we have failed to properly understand the complex relationships between them. It is also possible to misunderstand temporary evolutionary developments which may actually work well, if they are not interfered with. Our knowledge is improving all the time, but there remains much that we simply do not understand. Nature is a wondrous and complex mechanism, after all.

The primary deficiency in our approach is surely the narrowness of focus that we bring to bear upon a given situation. This may often be due to a particular bias or assumption with which an initiative is formulated, coupled to a lack of appreciation of the broader scenario. Within international academia, we have developed a great deal of detailed and very well researched knowledge. How much of this knowledge effectively finds its way to practical initiatives is questionable. Even within academia, it may often be fragmented and uncoordinated. Even worse, elements of it may be selected and deliberately misconstrued in order to serve parochial or political agendas. Selective media representation may serve to accentuate such a situation. Consequently, for new initiatives striving to take the best possible approach, arriving at a correct understanding of the broader scenario may prove more difficult than supposed. This may particularly be the case if the initiative is under-supported at both regional and national levels.

Often, we don't seem to achieve a practical coordination of effort and the harnessing of related expertise. For example population geneticists have undertaken a good deal of valuable research, as have biologists, geologists and conservationists, all of which may serve to inform across boundaries and help to develop a more robust understanding. However, such undertakings have too often been undertaken in isolation, with the results not necessarily shared or correlated across boundaries of operation and research. This is not a criticism of the agencies involved, but rather an acknowledgement of a missed opportunity. One way of potentially improving upon this situation is to promote the use of a common language with which to describe what we see around us and how it is changing over time. We shall explore this ides elsewhere within this volume. This approach, in turn might aid a practical coordination whereby, even if the lower level research adopts a different complexion within its detail, the results might be expressed in alignment with a commonly understood broader framework. In order to understand why this is important, we need look no further than the various disparate systems adopted at a national level and operable within national boundaries. A further dichotomy exists between the language of mathematical models often constructed in order to explain past and present realities and the practical orchestration of an informed, strategic vision for the future. And yet, the two might usefully work together within such a strategy.

Naturally, there is much that we have yet to understand, across many boundaries of both geography and scientific discipline, including the evolutionary factors at work within all natural habitats and ecosystems. However, the development of a better coordinated approach might serve to accelerate our understanding, thus leading to a more effective practical orchestration of our conservation efforts at every scale. The consequent enhanced observation, understanding and coordination will serve us well from a practical perspective.

The implications of our approach

If we do not manage to achieve a more unified and correlated approach to conservation, we shall run the risk of creating a plethora of localised initiatives that simply do not work together for the common conservationist good. Indeed, in some areas, we may actually make things worse by triggering or otherwise accelerating an evolutionary response which is not in the broader interest. We are beginning to understand the sometimes highly complex interactions and dependencies across habitats and between species. Yet we often fail to acknowledge the same within independent conservation initiatives. Sometimes, the protection of a single species without reference to this broader web of complexities, may prove harmful in the longer term to both the broader habitat and, ironically, to the species concerned. In particular, our understanding of evolution and evolutionary responses in association with the aforementioned interactions and dependencies, needs to be robust when we consider the plight of a given species within one or more of these habitats. However, such a robustness of understanding is not always the case. Consequently, we run the risk of meddling with a broader framework which we do not properly understand.

The natural world and its evolutionary model encompass a capacity for adaptation and compensatory response which, if allowed to function, will generally find a balance. Whether this balance meets with our aesthetic appreciation is another matter of course. However, if we interfere with this balance, with an incomplete knowledge of the mechanisms involved, then the outcome might be unpredictable. Our understanding of this reality should be driving us towards a better coordination of our established expertise across disciplines and cultures. Without such a coordination, we shall remain uncertain of the longer term implications of individual initiatives. This is surely not a desirable outcome given the need to protect our natural world altogether.

We might usefully consider some related factors and ask some pertinent questions as follows;

Should our focus be on saving individual species or on protecting the evolutionary process? The two aims are not always compatible. Within the greater evolutionary model there is a degree of species alignment, with some species becoming extinct and others prospering according to the prevailing conditions. This is perfectly natural and reflects the mechanism that has been working successfully on our planet for many millions of years. As such, it is something which, perhaps, we should not interfere with too much. No doubt there will be mixed views in this context, depending upon the habitats and species in question.

We should also be wary of separating humanity from nature. We have tended to consider ourselves somewhat separate from the natural world, with the expectancy that we can control it according to our whims or perceived requirements. Some would hold that we can control, or even replace nature with science and technology. Certainly we can have a significant impact upon natural processes and can even interfere with the genetic model in order to serve our designs. However, we must also acknowledge that we are ourselves an integral component of nature, the natural world and natural evolutionary processes. Shall we ever control those processes completely? It seems unlikely, given our rudimentary knowledge and nature's adaptive capacity. Surely a better approach would be to work with nature, rather than trying to control or conquer it. To endeavour to understand how we might best interact with the complex web of natural processes that define our beautiful world.

We are beginning to understand the interactions and dependencies across different spatial and temporal environments, although we could usefully strive to weave a stronger evolutionary thread into this awareness, in order to understand the effect of such changes on adaptive response. Indeed, without this understanding of evolutionary mechanisms, our various conservation initiatives must necessarily be rendered as mere temporary measures. In particular, we must consider the effects of habitat fragmentation and dispersal and how this effects population dynamics, including the ability to adapt. An organisms fitness may only be evaluated with reference to its environment at a given point in time and its environment is subject to change to varying degrees. Consequently, habitat fragmentation and destruction effectively limits speciation as the time needed for adaptation is cut short. This is all part of the broader evolutionary process, of which we are an integral component and upon which we are undoubtedly having a significant effect. It is important to understand this bigger picture and allow this understanding to inform our decisions around conservation at local scales. This is a key objective of the Evolutionary Conservation initiative.

In short, our definition of conservation must be expanded to include evolutionary factors, as well as an understanding of interactions, relationships and dependencies across boundaries. Without such an expanded definition, we run the risk of limiting the effectiveness of our endeavours, however well intentioned they may be. Furthermore, this expanded definition needs to be aligned with a practical mechanism for knowledge sharing and a means of disseminating information to all who might benefit from it, irrespective of geography, culture or politics. Within the pages of this volume, such a mechanism will be discussed in some detail.

Summary

In this chapter we have discussed conservation in broad terms and as is generally understood today. We started by considering the origins of conservation which, initially, had little to do with the welfare of our planet and more to do with the selfish desires of a relatively small number of privileged individuals. We have also acknowledged the segmentation of land for political and cultural reasons, rather than for any reasons of conservation. All such activities have had an impact upon our world and its habitats as we perceive them today. The appreciation of the beauty of nature in its own right has been reflected in the arts for as long as man has been able to record his thoughts, but particularly within later landscape painting, poetry and even literature. This appreciation has perhaps, in some ways, served to inform an increasing scientific interest which, in turn, has been reflected in related activities, the formation of national parks representing an example, as acknowledged herein.

We have additionally examined the definition of conservation as popularly understood and acknowledged the political and commercial factors which become entangled with such a definition. Similarly, from an academic perspective, there are often other factors which serve to confuse the whole.

There is consequently a need for a more pure, universally accepted understanding and broad based definition, together with related methodologies which may support the same. The part played by government agencies adopts a special importance in this respect and this has been acknowledged, as has the need to take a longer term perspective, based upon solid scientific principles and good research. In this vein, we have continued to look at conservation in practice and some potential deficiencies in our current approach. These include the tendency to take too parochial a view, often in ignorance of the broader perspective. We have looked at the implications of current practices and suggested the need for a better coordination of effort, giving some examples of related factors in order to illustrate this requirement. In short, this chapter has served to take a brief look at conservation as currently understood and practised before we progress to an introduction to the concept of Evolutionary Conservation and why it has been proposed.

4. Evolutionary Conservation

Abstract

The concept of Evolutionary Conservation is introduced in this chapter as an alternative approach to conservation as typically practised. We discuss the sheer scale of species and the complex web of dependencies and interactions which exist between them and the natural environments that they inhabit as they all play their part within the larger tapestry of life. We move on to discuss species diversity and adaptation via the processes of evolution, explaining why it is important to understand this evolutionary picture within the context of conservation and how the Evolutionary Conservation model facilitates such an understanding. In a similar vein, we explore the parameters of time and space and place our current evolutionary situation within an even broader context, emphasising that conservation without reference to evolution is in itself of an unnecessarily constrained value. We also emphasise the importance of critical observation and, in particular, the broad and timely observation necessary in order to support the concept of Evolutionary Conservation and create the wider understanding facilitated by that model. We discuss the need for coordination at a practical level and how the Evolutionary Conservation model supports the collection and sharing of information for the common good, using simple, intuitive tools which may easily be used by specialists and enthusiasts alike. This chapter consequently provides a brief overview of the Evolutionary Conservation model, the details of which will be expanded upon in subsequent chapters.

Introduction

Let us, for a moment, consider the smaller scale. All of the tiny creatures and organisms which we can barely see and yet which account for a huge number of species. In the fauna alone, we know of around one and a half million species and it has been estimated that there might exist somewhere between ten and two hundred million separate species overall. In the aquatic world, among the tiny creatures, we have the ctenophore, porifera, placazoa, cnidaria, cephalochordate, tunicate, echinodermata, xenoturbellida, acoelomorpha, chaetognatum and many other groupings. In the terrestrial world we have the amazing arthropods in all their bizarre and beautiful forms, all the little creatures that live in the soil and leaf litter and much more besides. Every one of these little animals is dependant upon a combination of its fellow creatures and the environment in which it finds itself. Moreover, every one of these little animals has a specific part to play within the greater orchestration of life on Earth. As we turn our attention towards the larger, more easily discernible creatures, the complex web of dependencies continues to grow. Now let us add the flora and the various environments, habitats and the complexity of atmospheric and chemical conditions within each ecosystem, at every scale. If we could take a simple snapshot in time of this great web of dependencies and interactions, it would doubtless prove to be beyond our comprehension. And yet such a snapshot, valuable as it may be, would take no account of the dynamic mechanisms of evolution which serve to further complicate the situation. To understand, even at a rudimentary level, this extraordinary and beautiful tapestry of life and its myriad interactions is a task almost unimaginable. It is possible that the human species itself will become extinct long before such an understanding could ever be reached. The best we can do is to try to live in harmony with this wondrous entity, which we call the natural world, for as long as possible. To do so, we must observe this world very carefully and strive to understand our observations in a coordinated manner across boundaries of geography, politics and culture, in order that we may at least sketch that broader, most beautiful tapestry. This is the underlying premise of Evolutionary Conservation. To facilitate the development of that sketch; a sketch which, in turn, will inform the development of a much deeper understanding of our world and how best to protect it.

Mounting conservation initiatives in order to save a single species, or to maintain a given habitat in a manner which is aesthetically pleasing to ourselves is not enough. We must take the broader perspective and all its complexities into account, regardless of our precise location on planet Earth. To do so, we must be cognisant of other situations and be able to interpret them in a uniform manner in order to develop this broader perspective. The concept of Evolutionary Conservation provides for this via a common classification and data collation method which allows for an increasingly rich understanding to be systematically developed at local, regional, national and international levels. Information collected at a series of local sites may be subsumed into a regional understanding. A collection of regional views may be subsumed into a national understanding and national perspectives may be subsumed into an international understanding, all using the same language and a common classification system. In order for such a scheme to remain practical, it must be positioned at a high enough level to be easily used by a wide cross section of agencies and individuals, while exposing enough detail to be meaningful. The Evolutionary Conservation model is consequently designed to sit comfortably within such a framework. In practice, it consists of a small set of tools supported by intuitive documentation, the classification system and a series of databases. With these simple tools, we may systematically create an unparalleled perspective of our world, ensuring that specific conservation initiatives are far better informed and thus more likely to be successful.

The great diversity

Diversity among species is both complex and volatile. We cannot encapsulate it within a time bubble and the degree to which we might exercise a control over it may ultimately be limited, although we should do everything we can to support and maintain species diversity. After all, prolonging diversity on Earth will ultimately prolong our own existence. However, the evolutionary component of species diversity is complex. Species may develop and adapt in relation to their particular environment, whether this be a micro habitat or a more free ranging area, but this adaptation may not always result in a greater sophistication of either form or behaviour. Indeed, there are many examples of species evolving to a simpler level and discarding attributes in order to better adapt to changing conditions. In addition, among this ever changing kaleidoscope of evolution, some species are destined for extinction while others are maintained, created or heavily adapted. This is the way it has always been and is the natural way of things. Without this ability to discard and renew, species evolution may not be able to keep pace with changing conditions. Indeed, species themselves contribute to the ever changing habitats and conditions upon planet Earth. The human species has brought about significant changes within a relatively short period of time. Consequently, we must expect an evolutionary reaction. This will undoubtedly entail a number of species becoming extinct as they struggle to adapt to these changes. Such an extinction event may not be immediate and may take many generations as given populations fail to maintain their numbers and move slowly towards the inevitable. We should understand that, in order for species to survive, their habitats and the species diversity within them, which in turn provide for the necessary interactions and dependencies, must also survive. If habitats change slowly and naturally over time, species may have an opportunity to adapt accordingly. When habitats are more quickly fragmented or destroyed by anthropological action, then there is often no time to adapt and extinction will be the result for many species. This is inevitable. It may therefore be posited that habitat destruction is the enemy of evolution and species diversity. In between the extremes there exist a number of volatile situations caused by the ever spiralling numbers of humans and the ensuing development that this entails. We are, in fact, an integral component within the larger evolutionary model, for better or for worse.

To understand species diversity in its entirety, even within the confines of a defined habitat, is a significant undertaking which, in many instances, will be beyond the capacity of those involved. However, for the purposes of sympathetic conservation, it may be enough to be able to observe changes in local species diversity and, consequently, begin to understand the causes for such changes. In such a manner we may ensure that our conservation efforts are both realistic and in alignment with natural processes, while being subject to continual monitoring. This is where the concept of Evolutionary Conservation, as proposed in this work, can prove invaluable, not only at the localised level, but as a means to align local, regional and national environments in order to appreciate the broader perspective. The Ecogram mechanism allows for both diversity and change over time to be monitored and documented at every level. This, in turn, allows us to systematically develop an understanding of the broader picture and place species diversity and evolutionary change within a proper perspective. This is important if we are to inform individual conservation initiatives properly. Species do not exist in isolation. They rely upon each other as well as their particular habitats. This applies to us also. Maintaining natural habitats and the diversity of species which they support is very much in our own interest. Surely much more so than the short term gain typically enjoyed as a result of habitat destruction. In the interests of ongoing civilisation, we should be taking such matters into careful consideration.

Time and space

An interesting concept to consider is that of scale, especially scale in evolutionary terms. We might start by thinking of the universe itself and the position of our galaxy, the Milky Way, within that universal space. Theories abound as to the creation of the universe and the evolutionary formation of our galaxy. Within that galaxy, at another scale, we have the evolution of our sun and its family of orbiting planets within our solar system. This entire system has evolved over time, including the accumulation of rotating debris and gases which formed the planets in their particular juxtapositions according to their composition. Our own planet came to occupy a unique position, just the right distance from the sun, wherein the conditions existed for an equally unique evolution at the local level. Before we even think about the evolution of biological life on Earth, there is an entire evolutionary spectrum which has occurred in order to create the perfect conditions for the creation of that biological life. We might almost think of this as an evolutionary continuum within which the creation of biological life is but a step along the way. Following this, we have the important steps of cell division and the leap from single cell organisms to the multi cellular life which would itself unlock an almost unlimited set of evolutionary possibilities. Further significant steps along this evolutionary continuum included the development of sensory organs, the development of limbs and body plans and, of course, the point at which life emerged from the oceans to colonise our terrestrial Earth. Before we consider conservation at local levels, we might usefully remind ourselves of the long and fascinating evolutionary path that has lead us to this current position. We might also consider that the evolutionary journey is far from over and is continuing along its path, with us, currently, as an integral component. How this unfolds for the projected life of our solar system is another matter, worthy of our contemplation. With respect to the spatial domain, we may have little effective influence at universal or galactic scales, but we can strive to understand our own planet and the complex web of interactions and dependencies that exist upon it. Bringing the two domains of time and space together at our planetary level, we may further consider how the hydrosphere, geosphere and atmosphere have followed their own evolutionary journey in order to create just the right conditions for the formation of the biosphere and how, consequently, they all continue to evolve and interact together in both the spatial and temporal domains. Such considerations pave the way for us to think about the concept of Evolutionary Conservation in a practical manner.

In contrast, one of the potential issues with current conservation initiatives is a tendency to be parochial in their focus. Very often, they are concerned with the preservation of a single species or a single, narrowly defined habitat. Furthermore, many initiatives are undertaken in a 'snapshot' manner whereby they focus their research and resultant understanding across a narrowly defined time period. Consequently, measures which may have been useful at a particular point in time may cease to be so at a later point, due to other developments or unforeseen natural reactions. Conservation is not something that may be applied, like a sticking plaster, and then forgotten. If we are to really protect our natural habitats and the species that they contain, then conservation must be an ongoing, full time undertaking. Every situation must be constantly monitored and any changes understood within both a local and broader context. Just as with the development of the human race, where our history and relative wellbeing has been inter linked over the millennia, the same is true of the natural world, a world in which we remain an integral part. The Evolutionary Conservation model holds the promise of being able to provide this bigger picture across boundaries of time and space. By a process of continual monitoring and correlation across local, regional and national boundaries, we may begin to understand local situations in a broader context. Furthermore, by looking both backwards and forwards in time, we may begin to understand the broader evolutionary picture as well. This is, in fact, critically important with respect to the efficacy of our conservation efforts at every turn. Conservation without reference to evolution becomes increasingly meaningless over time. And time is not on our side. The rate with which the human species is affecting the world around us is unprecedented and we simply do not comprehend the complexity or potential scale of natural reactions. We desperately need to bring the evolutionary factor into our deliberations around conservation.

Similarly, we need to start seeing conservation as a global requirement for the wellbeing of our planet as a whole. Focusing on specific, local situations simply does not achieve this, however well-meaning some of those efforts may be. We must start to understand the broader spatial perspective and its implications. In order to do this, we need a common mechanism and, as far as is practicable, a common language, with which we may quickly embark upon the development of this broader perspective. Furthermore, we should not limit the gathering of the necessary information to established scientists operating within specific domains, but should find a way to broaden this task out to a wider range of individuals, whether they be government agency workers or secondary school students, in order that we may develop our broader understanding as quickly as possible. These two dimensions of space and time must be incorporated into our global conservation model if it is to have a positive impact upon the trajectory of evolution within the time frame of human civilisation. If we fail to achieve this, our parochial conservation initiatives will become little more than minor diversions from a destiny which we do not properly understand. Adopting a broader perspective will help us to place local initiatives in a proper context and beyond the aesthetic ideal which we sometimes impose upon such matters, an ideal which is itself subject to change. We cannot lock habitats in a time capsule, we must allow them to breath and evolve in a mutually sympathetic manner. For this, we need to develop our understanding of the broader picture.

Developing such a comprehension is a goal of the Evolutionary Conservation concept, and the tools which it provides are geared to support this goal, including an intuitive ease of use which may apply across boundaries of geography, politics and culture. Provision is made for every participating habitat to undertake an annual audit, using the tools provided, effectively developing the local understanding systematically, year on year, while extrapolating this understanding on a spatial basis in order to simultaneously develop a broader geographic perspective. This concept may be extrapolated to an international and, ultimately, global level. The result will be the systematic development of a rich tapestry of understanding which may be freely shared among all in order to inform conservation initiatives at every level, wherever they may be. Within this broad tapestry, individual research projects may continue to develop our understanding at lower levels, feeding into the common good of knowledge around species and natural processes. The Evolutionary Conservation model will sit at a higher level, spanning such activities across geographical, cultural and political boundaries. It is, in fact, complementary to all the good research being undertaken within academia, government agencies or specialist organisations across our world.

Observation

Given the above, it becomes clear that critical observation has a key part to play within this endeavour. Furthermore, this observation is required upon a broad scale and according to a uniform methodology which allows for it to be shared across boundaries. In many specific fields and associated habitats, we have already undertaken very detailed observations in order to understand equally specific situations. While proving extremely valuable at the time, these observations can become out of step with reality if they are not maintained. However, maintaining them at such a level, and across wide areas, is not always practically feasible. We need to find a way of maintaining observation, perhaps at a higher level, across wide areas in order to properly understand evolutionary change. To accomplish such a task, we need to engage a larger number of individuals who, via the use of intuitive tools, can undertake such an observation on a continued basis. In addition, such an undertaking should be widely distributed, throughout every land and region possible in order to create our broader understanding. Positioning this observation at exactly the right level is a challenge. If too low a level is suggested, the observation will be restricted to a smaller number of entities and individuals who may understand this lower level. Consequently, the observations will rarely be undertaken in a timely fashion or maintained, as it will prove too difficult to do so. Furthermore, their spatial distribution will be limited. On the other hand, if positioned at too high a level, the observations will have a more limited value. At the right level, our widely distributed observations will feed into and inform the broader understanding, suggesting areas where a lower level of research would clearly be beneficial. This in itself would be truly useful. In addition, these distributed and maintained observations will provide an ongoing correlation factor which will prove extremely useful in the understanding of the broader situation and its complex web of interactions and dependencies.

To achieve this ideal, we need to motivate and mobilise a large number of individuals capable of making the necessary observations and capturing them in a uniform manner. We need, in fact, a veritable, international army of Evolutionary Conservation practitioners. Such an army may be readily recruited from the ranks of appropriate government agencies, academic research, enthusiastic volunteers, community initiatives and, perhaps, secondary schools. In the latter case, the Evolutionary Conservation model may serve a dual purpose of feeding into our broader understanding while simultaneously introducing young students to the Earth sciences and the importance of conservation, helping future generations perhaps to take a more sympathetic approach towards a global conservation initiative. Indeed, one could imagine some wonderful educational programmes being constructed around the use of the Evolutionary Conservation model in schools. An ambitious idea perhaps, but an idea which is entirely realisable, if we have the will to pursue it.

The Ecogram template provides the basis for the uniform observation required for our objective. It may be used as a paper form, an electronic form or as a portable database with direct data entry. Most probably, an initial set of paper or electronic forms will be coordinated into a single database entry for a given location and associated habitat. The exercise of completing the observations and posting the database record will be undertaken annually at each defined location, providing for an increasingly rich understanding to be formed, year on year, including around evolutionary change and associated trends. At an individual point of presence, this understanding will be systematically developed in a manner which has hitherto proved impossible in most cases, due to a lack of a uniform continuity across time. The Ecogram provides the necessary uniformity of approach and will be described more fully in a subsequent chapter. At the regional level and above, annual Summary Statements provide a mechanism by which important trends may be identified and captured, additional observations made and appropriate conclusions being formed. Additional tools are provided for capturing the spatial distribution of species where important. The Evolutionary Conservation practitioner has everything they need to capture relevant information at a variety of levels, according to the situation at hand. This is valuable enough in isolation, but becomes increasingly valuable when this information is shared in the interests of the common good.

Coordination

For conservation to work in practice and at the broader scale, we need a certain coordination of both understanding and practical effort. Typically, such a coordination is easy enough to realise at a local scale, but becomes increasingly difficult across boundaries. A large part of this is political and results from a lack of agreement and effective coordination, in spite of a myriad of international summits and conferences where such matters are discussed ad infinitum by an army of ministers, specialists and advisors. Part of the problem is also rooted in fundamental differences of culture which are often not well understood with respect to specific initiatives and, of course, the picture is additionally confused by commerce and the industry which has grown around ecological issues. What is needed is some sort of coordinating focus. Something to which all parties may subscribe while retaining their independence in other matters. Evolutionary Conservation provides such a focus with a model which is universal, intuitive in use, scalable to a global level and freely available to all. Furthermore, it allows for and supports a practical coordination at every level, from local, through regional and national, to international. Yet it is more than simply a practical mechanism. It is indeed a philosophy – a new way of thinking about conservation and its importance to the wellbeing of both our planet and of human civilisation altogether. An acknowledgement of the need to understand the broader perspective and to share this understanding for the common good. Consequently, effective coordination is key to the concept of Evolutionary Conservation.

The interesting thing is that, while the Evolutionary Conservation mechanism provides for a practical coordination at every level, it also allows for this coordination to evolve systematically as increasing numbers of participants practice the methodology. It is in itself an evolutionary component. However, the will to participate and coordinate will be crucial to the success of the concept, just as it is with any such endeavour. As time passes, it will therefore be important to communicate the Evolutionary Conservation concept and encourage others to adopt it. In such a manner, coordination will grow and blossom, from small beginnings to something more pervasive and increasingly effective. Ideally, we shall need a single coordinating point for all related endeavours as individual groups and areas experiment with the methodology. Initially, the author will support this requirement although, ultimately, an independent entity will need to be found who can perform this central coordination task on an ongoing basis. A key part of this task will lie in the maintenance and dissemination of the broader perspective previously referred to. However, even in the absence of such an entity, coordination may take place at every level, orchestrated by implementing agencies and individual initiatives alike. If we are to take conservation to the next level, then coordination must play a primary part within our endeavours.

Practical conservation

Practical conservation is a multi-faceted undertaking, often requiring specialist skills at a variety of levels. Understanding precisely why a given situation is developing in a particular manner requires an understanding of all the variables involved. This, in turn, usually requires the coordination of specialist skills with respect to the habitats and species involved. However, if such skills are brought to bear on a temporary basis, as often happens for the course of a particular initiative, then the conclusions reached will be based upon a 'snapshot in time' view of the situation which may or may not prove to be correct over the longer term. Furthermore, when the initiative has concluded and the specialists have returned to other endeavours, those remaining may not understand what to look for in order to confirm that everything is on track. In reality, few habitats enjoy the luxury of full time specialists covering all of the areas concerned. Actions taken in one area may have unpredictable consequences in another, which only specialists in that area might understand, and this situation extends beyond the host habitat to surrounding areas. In practice, situations may become quite complex and this complexity is in itself a variable, changing and developing in response to the broader situation.

A different approach would be to instigate a higher level, continuous monitoring activity which notices changes and can compare a given situation with other habitats in adjacent areas or areas of similar conditions elsewhere. Conclusions could then be quickly reached and, where applicable, specialist skills brought in to confirm the situation. Over time, and for a given area, the systematically developed detailed knowledge would suffice to manage the habitat successfully with little outside assistance. Neighbouring habitats would similarly develop a detailed understanding which could be shared among all those in the area for the common good. The practice could extend to neighbouring areas and even further afield, creating an in depth understanding of the broader perspective. This is one of the tenets of the Evolutionary Conservation model. To provide a framework within which this continuous monitoring may take place in a uniform manner, using common classifications in order that a broader understanding may be developed and easily shared across boundaries. An integral part of this continuous monitoring is an effective log of changes observed and actions taken, together with scheduled actions into the future based upon the current understanding. In such a manner, a detailed scenario is created piece by piece, year by year, which brings a clarity and focus to bear which may easily be understood by all concerned, including those who might be new to a given area or initiative. This sort of rich information rarely exists today and, where something like it does exist, it is usually presented in a parochial manner which has little relevance outside of the core initiative and is therefore not easily understood in a broader context. Consequently, the Evolutionary Conservation methodology has much to offer the broader community. In particular, it provides for an evolutionary perspective to be developed at every level, ensuring that this perspective is continually enhanced as localised nodes share information across the spatial domain. In addition, the Evolutionary Conservation concept may be of great value in an educational sense, encouraging a wider appreciation of conservation issues.

Summary

In this chapter, we have explored the concept of Evolutionary Conservation as an alternative approach to conservation in general. We started by considering the multitude of life which exists upon our Earth and acknowledging the complex web of relationships, interactions and dependencies within this greater evolutionary picture. We similarly acknowledged the difficulty in understanding this greater picture across both temporal and spatial domains and stressed the importance of a systematic programme of observation, as might be facilitated by the Evolutionary Conservation model, in order to build this greater understanding. We went on to look at species diversity and the evolutionary processes which allowed for adaptation and the creation of that rich diversity, stressing that, in order to understand diversity within the context of a given habitat, we must also understand something of the evolutionary position with respect to that habitat. Furthermore, we should ideally understand this in relation to neighbouring habitats and, ultimately, the broader global perspective.

Evolution operates across both time and space and is itself broader than simply a question of biological life on Earth. We considered this from the broader perspective of the creation of the Earth itself and the evolutionary path which lead, eventually, to just the right conditions for biological life to be triggered. When considering this broader scale, the suggestion that our current evolutionary position is simply a notch along a longer path leading far into the future, tends to place evolution and species diversity into perspective. This in turn emphasises the futility of taking too parochial a view towards conservation. Indeed, conservation without reference to evolution has limited value in real terms and this is an important point to take into consideration. This is precisely why the Evolutionary Conservation concept allows for a rolling, systematic observation which will build this evolutionary picture while simultaneously looking both backward and forward with respect to every habitat captured within this model.

In order to pursue our goals, observation clearly has a major part to play. However, we need to align observation with the reality of our expectations and, consequently, support a much broader observational model. We discussed how this might be positioned at a higher level, allowing for a collaboration between specialist scientists and non specialist enthusiasts and practitioners, in order to more quickly develop our broader understanding. The Ecogram and Summary Statement templates will be the key to facilitating this wider observational model. We also discussed the need for coordination and how, in spite of a myriad of international conferences and government initiatives, practical coordination remains relatively weak. We suggested that an independent focus such as Evolutionary Conservation, which has absolutely no political or commercial bias, might provide a better vehicle for such a coordination. The Evolutionary Conservation database tool will be particularly useful in this context, as will the Ecogram with its use of common classification codes across a wide range of parameters. We concluded by looking at practical conservation and how a wider dissemination of information, coupled to a programme of continuous monitoring would bring benefits in this area. Such an approach would obviate against a lack of specialist skills on a continual basis and the 'snapshot in time' approach which is often taken to conservation. In all these areas, the Evolutionary Conservation model brings potential advantages as it facilitates the creation and dissemination of a much broader perspective. In addition, it is scalable and intuitive in use, making it an easy matter to adopt the methodology for all conservation initiatives, whether orchestrated by government agencies, academia, community enterprise or individually inspired projects. This chapter has consequently set the scene for the discussion of a new approach to conservation. In the next chapter, we shall take a closer look at the Ecogram, the primary tool used within the Evolutionary Conservation model.

5. Introducing the Ecogram

Abstract

This chapter provides an introduction to the Ecogram, the key component within the Evolutionary Conservation model. We explain the concept and the associated benefits of this model, before moving on to explain each of the sections within the Ecogram, and all of their respective fields. We further explain the distinction between using the classification codes and the free-form text fields. We emphasise that, while ostensibly a simple and intuitive mechanism, the Ecogram is, in fact, a very powerful tool within our conservation tool set. This is necessarily a short chapter, simply to introduce the model. Practitioners may like to experiment with the Ecogram in order to gain experience and understand how best to use it within their particular sphere of operation.

Introduction

The Ecogram, as has been mentioned in previous chapters, is the primary tool with which to support the concept of Evolutionary Conservation. It is simple and intuitive in use, and yet granular enough to capture observations of real value to conservation initiatives at every scale, a factor which is crucially important to the broader concept. Furthermore, it provides for a continual monitoring approach to be executed with respect to natural habitats at any scale, thus providing the basis for a systematic development of knowledge including, very importantly, an understanding of the evolutionary forces acting upon that habitat. When this knowledge is shared across habitats and related operations, an even greater understanding may be developed, encompassing aspects of interaction and dependency which form a part of that broader evolutionary model. As expertise is shared across the broader boundaries of geography, politics and culture, an even richer understanding is developed with respect to the broader tapestry of life upon Earth. All of this from the humble Ecogram, itself nothing more than a simple document containing a structure of fields for capturing information in a uniform manner. Indeed, it is this simple elegance which renders the

Ecogram such a potentially powerful tool, as it is easily used by a wide cross section of practitioners from accomplished scientists to enthusiastic amateurs, all of whom may contribute to the broader understanding facilitated by this model..

The Ecogram may be used as a paper document in the field or may be accessed as a file on a portable computing device. There may be several variations of approach, depending upon the precise initiative and who is involved in its orchestration. Alternatively, Ecogram information may be entered directly into the Evolutionary Conservation database (which shall be explored within a subsequent chapter), which also may be run on a relatively low powered portable computing device. In practice, individuals will probably make notes in the field and then come back to base and consolidate these notes within an Ecogram document held as a computer file. A series of such documents may then be transferred to the database when convenient. The document will itself be a living entity as individuals collect information and append salient points into the Ecogram. Each document, for each defined area, will be consolidated and finalised once per year and it is this final representation which will be entered into the database. One could therefore consider the Ecogram as a culmination of the years conservation research for a particular habitat. Once the document has been finalised and entered into the database, this database file will be sent to the next hierarchical level where it will be subsumed into a larger database of Ecograms representing a broader area. It is, in fact, an integral component within a broader information architecture. The defined hierarchical areas are that of local initiative, regional area, national, international (or continental) and, eventually, global. Nature herself operates upon a global level with regional distinctions, down to precise local habitats and ecosystems, and so it follows that our understanding should be equally broad and detailed in order to support our various conservation initiatives, wherever they may exist and upon whatever scale, hence the Ecogram and associated structure. Later in this work, the reader will discover exactly how this structure may operate in a unified, fully coordinated manner in order to systematically develop and share this detailed understanding.

However, for now, the remainder of this chapter will explore the different Ecogram sections, their overall purpose and the detail of the information captured within them. The Ecogram should be used in conjunction with the Evolutionary Conservation classification system which is expressed in the form of a simple spreadsheet. This spreadsheet contains the codes necessary for completion of various sections of the Ecogram, together with their meaning. The database already has the classification system embedded into it, in order that the various codes may be easily and quickly selected.

The Ecogram sections are as follows;

Metadata

The first section of the Ecogram is devoted to the collection of primary information, or metadata, about the habitat or ecosystem in question. This information is in itself very useful, especially when many Ecogram records are collected into an Evolutionary Conservation database. The various fields and their purpose within the metadata section are described as follows;

Ecogram ID

This is a unique identifier for each Ecogram record. It consists of an eleven character string with the first three characters representing the country code (according to the international standard), the next two characters representing the region, the next two characters representing the particular locale, the next two characters a numeric identifier of the Ecogram for that locale (there may be more than one Ecogram record for a locale) and the final two characters representing the year for that particular record. An example might be CANBLNB0114 where the country is Canada, the region British Columbia and the locale Nass Basin, this being Ecogram number one in the year 2014. A simple, yet effective, naming convention which will quickly become second nature to practitioners.

Organisation

This is simply the name of the organisation completing the Ecogram. It may be a government agency, an academic department, a charitable organisation, a specialist conservation group, a school or a community.

Country

The country to which the Ecogram appertains.

Region

The region within the country to which the Ecogram appertains. This may be the name of a state, county or other defined region.

Locale

The particular locality to which the Ecogram appertains. This may be a defined habitat or area which is easily recognisable.

Latitude

The latitude which best defines the centre of the locale. This may be expressed simply in degrees and minutes, such as 23°26' N or in full notation, such as 23°26'10" N.

Longitude

The longitude which best defines the centre of the locale. This may be expressed simply in degrees and minutes, such as 34°15' E   or in full notation, such as 34°15'23" E

Area

The approximate area described by the Ecogram, expressed in square kilometres (Km²).

Primary Habitat

The primary habitat of this area, expressed as a four character code, as defined by the Evolutionary Conservation classification system.

Base Geology

The base geology underpinning this area, expressed as a four character code, as defined by the Evolutionary Conservation classification system.

Substrate

The finer substrate exposed within this area, expressed as a four character code, as defined by the Evolutionary Conservation classification system.

Topography

The overall topography of this area, expressed as a four character code, as defined by the Evolutionary Conservation classification system.

Elevation

The average elevation of this area, expressed as a four character code, as defined by the Evolutionary Conservation classification system.

Prepared by

The name of the individual responsible for preparing the Ecogram. This will be useful when liaising across areas.

Year

The year to which the Ecogram appertains. An Ecogram is prepared every year for a given location.

Contact

The primary contact details, usually an email address, for this particular Ecogram.

The combination of items within the metadata section provides an overview of the area being covered by the Ecogram. This supports analysis when multiple Ecogram records are present within an Evolutionary Conservation database.

Dynamic data

The dynamic data section is, in many ways, the heart of the Ecogram. It captures not only a snapshot in time of the current situation, but also evolutionary trends which, in turn, may provide an early warning of developing situations. Furthermore, it encourages a forward thinking perspective by allowing predictions based upon past and present observations. In addition, it allows for the definition of dependencies and indicator species as well as environmental factors such as temperature and soil acidity.

This section is itself split into three areas: the main evolutionary matrix, the dependencies area and environmental factors. The combination provide a more detailed picture of the area covered by the Ecogram. Subsequent editions of the Ecogram for this particular habitat will capture changes in all these areas, providing and increasingly rich understanding of the area in question and how it is evolving over time. This continual monitoring in a uniform manner will also allow the consequences of conservation actions to be noticed and understood. Furthermore, this enriched understanding may easily be shared across boundaries, courtesy of the Evolutionary Conservation mechanism.

We start by looking at the evolutionary matrix. This provides for six distinct views to be formulated, plus an overall measurement of concern. The distinct views include one for the current year or present time, three for previous periods at ten, twenty five and fifty years in the past and two for future predictions at ten and twenty five years in the future. Information for the past time windows will usually be available with a little research, showing the development, or otherwise, over time for the distinct habitat covered by the Ecogram. The future time categories enable a prediction based on this knowledge. For each of these time windows and their overall concern rating, we have several categories, defined by the Evolutionary Conservation classification system codes as follows;

Habitat

A code representing the primary habitat for the area covered by this Ecogram.

Soil Coverage

An indication of the level of soil coverage for this area.

Species Diversity

An indication of the status of species diversity for the area.

Flora

An indication of the particular status of flora within the area.

Fauna

An indication of the particular status of fauna within the area.

Climate

The primary climatic conditions in the area covered by the Ecogram.

Air Quality

An indication of the status of air quality within the area.

Water Quality

An indication of the status of water quality within the area.

This evolutionary matrix, while simple in concept, actually provides a very useful picture of the dynamics present within a given environment. Correlation with other Ecograms may also provide advance warning of the development of negative trends. In addition, it provides an immediate picture of evolution over time which is easily understood by all practitioners, whether local or remotely based. This supports knowledge sharing to an unprecedented degree.

The next sub section is a smaller matrix which provides a statement of currently perceived dependencies and indicator species at three levels. The multiple levels allow for changes to be accommodated and trends to be spotted as successive Ecograms systematically develop an enhanced understanding of the area in question. The factors within this section are;

Dependencies

The primary dependencies expressed via the Evolutionary Conservation classification codes.

Primary Flora

The primary flora types as expressed via the Evolutionary Conservation classification codes.

Primary Fauna

The primary fauna types as expressed via the Evolutionary Conservation classification codes.

A separate section is provided where an indicator species and its current status may be described. This is particularly useful where a habitat or ecosystem is undergoing change and a reaction may be noted within a particular species. Such a reaction may be used to herald forthcoming change before it becomes too serious. Two fields are provided for this purpose.

Indicator Species

A free form field where noted indicator species may be registered.

Indicator Status

A free form field where the status, or stability of the chosen indicator species may be noted.

We then have a simple grid for capturing quarterly mean temperatures, in Celsius, together with an annual average (the database also has a useful Fahrenheit convertor). Finally, we have a field for capturing soil acidity as expressed via the Evolutionary Conservation classification codes which mirror standard pH values.

At this point, we have captured quite a rich picture of the habitat area covered by a particular Ecogram. A third party analysing this information may quickly form an understanding of the area as it currently exists, together with an appreciation of the evolutionary developments which have lead to the current situation. In addition, they have a view of predictions and concerns from the Ecogram creator, based upon this observed information. As years pass and subsequent Ecograms are produced for this area, the quality and depth of information will increase accordingly. Consequently, the continued use of the Evolutionary Conservation model will enrich the detailed understanding of our world significantly.

Specific data

Up until this point, the Ecogram has featured defined fields and a standardised series of classification codes in order to describe the habitat and species under consideration. This methodology represents an intuitive, practical and repeatable way of gathering information which is scalable across boundaries. Consequently, this approach facilitates data correlation, coordination and collaboration across geographic, political and cultural boundaries. However, the granularity of such an approach must be positioned at a relatively high level in order to support these objectives. Therefore it is impossible to cover every eventuality down to a very low level of detail, or to capture subjective evaluations, specific to a particular area. In order to cater for this requirement, the last section of the Ecogram (Specific Data) allows for free form textual descriptions to be entered for a number of categories as follows;

Environmental Particulars

This section is divided into terrestrial and aquatic sub sections and allows any particular details to be captured which are not adequately represented within the main Ecogram body. This may include current concerns, predictions for the future, suggestions for remediation and other information pertinent to the situation within the current year of the Ecogram.

Change

This section allows for notes to be made about observed changes. It is divided into two sub sections: past to present and present to future. This allows for evolutionary aspects of change to be covered and predictions made accordingly. As years pass, subsequent Ecograms may validate these predictions as they build into an enhanced understanding of the situation. Over time, the understanding of evolutionary factors and how they affect the area under consideration will be similarly enhanced.

Risks

The risks section is divided into four sub sections; general threats, species threats, dependencies and relationships. It allows for all of these factors to be described at an appropriate level of detail. Furthermore, the consideration of these factors, in light of the information already gathered within the Ecogram, helps to develop a broader understanding of the area under consideration. In addition, risks which may be particular to the area, such as poaching for example, may be described in some detail while being placed within the broader context.

Suggested Actions

This section is also divided into four sub sections; immediate, 5 years, 10 years, and 20 years. This enables remedial actions to be defined and planned into the future, based upon the information gathered within the Ecogram. It is important to introduce the concept of proper, medium and long term planning into our conservation aspirations. As variously observed within these pages, we cannot preserve habitats and ecosystems as a snapshot in time. We must work to a continuum in sympathy with natural processes and ensure that we are planning our activities well into the future. As successive Ecograms are developed, these future plans may be rationalised and validated accordingly, providing a continuous monitoring and fine tuning function. This, in turn, introduces an evolutionary element into practical conservation.

Conclusions

In this section, the Ecogram creator may express overall conclusions around the Ecogram for the particular area on a particular year, based upon past and present observations. This provides for a brief synopsis or summary of the situation which may be easily absorbed and compared to that of previous years, thus understanding how the particular area is developing. Further detail may then be referenced within the main body of the Ecogram.

The classification system

The Ecogram is itself underpinned by the Evolutionary Conservation classification system. This is a simple system of codes to represent different entities relevant to habitats, species and broader environments. The use of common codes ensures that the recording of such factors is common across both spatial domains and, indeed, even spoken language, while also offering succinctness from a data recording perspective. In addition, the system is modular and easily extendible, providing flexibility and scalability into the future. Consequently, the Evolutionary Conservation model may be refined over time in order to position it at the optimum level for the broadest usage across boundaries, thus facilitating coordination and collaboration – themselves key tenets of the Evolutionary Conservation concept.

In practical terms, the classification system is expressed as a series of grouped codes and associated descriptions within a simple spreadsheet which may easily be referenced during the completion of an Ecogram. It is also echoed within the Evolutionary Conservation database, within which the codes and descriptions may be selected from drop down dialogues for easy data entry, and may be extrapolated to all manner of mobile computing devices as required. As and when the classification system is extended or otherwise revised, these tools will be updated and made freely available from a central source. However, such revisions should be a rare occurrence, the initial system being sufficiently robust for practical usage across a broad range of environments. In addition, it is acknowledged that the classification system is best kept simple, elegant and thus manageable. It is tempting to extrapolate down to increasingly lower levels of distinction and classification, however, such levels are not necessary to support the fundamental premise of Evolutionary Conservation. Consequently, modifications to the classification system should be infrequent. Practitioners are recommended to familiarise themselves with the classification system and its underlying logic, after which they will find it a fast and efficient mechanism for representing different aspects of a given habitat or ecosystem.

Summary

This chapter has been dedicated to the introduction of the Ecogram as the key instrument within the Evolutionary Conservation model. As such, it is important that practitioners become familiar with the Ecogram, the underlying classification system and the practical usage of the same. Within a given conservation initiative, a working methodology will no doubt be quickly arrived at in this context which suits and supports the situation at hand. We have covered the various sections of the Ecogram, explaining each field and its purpose accordingly. As indicated, many of these fields use the Ecogram codes as outlined in the classification system. This provides a degree of language independence, together with an efficient mechanism for data storage. Notwithstanding the logical structure of the Ecogram, there remains plenty of scope for a free-form expression of salient features, conditions and even views and predictions, via the specific data section. This allows for a systematic, year on year appraisal to be developed, leading to an increasingly rich understanding of the area in question. Together, the Ecogram, the classification system and the Evolutionary Conservation database model provide a complete, yet scalable structure for documenting and understanding our world, upon every scale. Furthermore, the components within this structure may easily be used by a broad cross section of individuals, irrespective of their particular discipline or experience. This enhances the potential scalability of the Evolutionary Conservation model.

The Ecogram, while primarily being an intuitive mechanism for data capture, is in fact something of a much greater significance. It introduces not only a practical methodology but a pathway into the very philosophy that lies at the heart of Evolutionary Conservation. The concept of observing and capturing information in a uniform and repeatable manner underpins the Evolutionary Conservation model. The intelligence thus gained may subsequently be shared throughout the Evolutionary Conservation community, both regionally and further afield, contributing to the creation of the broad tapestry of understanding referred to elsewhere within this volume. It is this shared and systematically enhanced understanding that will serve us well as we face the undoubted challenges that await us within 21st century life on Earth. The humble Ecogram is, in fact, an extremely powerful tool when properly understood and effectively deployed. We should distribute this power widely and embrace the knowledge and understanding that it provides for within the broader Evolutionary Conservation model.

6. Introducing the Summary Statement

Abstract

This is a very short chapter, the purpose of which is simply to introduce the concept of the Summary Statement. Consequently, we shall describe the mechanism and how it is used, explaining the individual information items and sections accordingly. In the summary to this chapter, we shall further explain the importance of the Summary Statement to the overall concept of Evolutionary Conservation.

Introduction

The Evolutionary Conservation concept relies upon observation and the gathering of detailed information, as explained in the previous chapter where we introduced the Ecogram and its purpose within the broader scheme of things. However, within such a methodology there has also to be room for a certain amount of interpretation, correlation and the summation of information into a concise overview; a sort of overture to preface the main performance. In such a manner, one who is not directly involved with local level initiatives may absorb the Summary Statement at a regional, national or higher level before drilling down to the detail of a specific Ecogram or series of Ecograms appertaining to the summary. Furthermore, Summary Statements may be used effectively to inform decision making or to feed into the creation of policies at various levels. They effectively extend the power and value of Evolutionary Conservation to a broader audience.

There is, of course, within the Ecogram itself, provision to capture summarised thoughts and conclusions with respect to the detail of that specific Ecogram. Consequently, there is no requirement for a Summary Statement at that local level. The benefits of summation appear at successively higher levels. from the regional and national, through to international and, ultimately, global. At each of these levels, scientific interpretation, the correlation of information and the alignment with other factors understood only at that level, may all come together in order to produce a cogent summary which may readily be understood and incorporated at even higher levels, as well as being made available to lower levels. In addition, these Summary Statements may be used by a variety of individuals and agencies, beyond the immediate Evolutionary Conservation community, to inform their own deliberations. One might envisage specific meetings or conferences where Summary Statements from the next level down in the operational hierarchy are presented and discussed prior to the creation of a Summary Statement at that level. It is indeed a parallel mechanism to the Ecogram which, while being synergistic, has a subtly different purpose. This rather short chapter discusses the Summary Statement and how it should be used.

Using the Summary Statement

The actuality of the Summary Statement and, in most cases, even its content, will be straightforward enough. However, careful consideration should be given to its completion and the use to which it will subsequently be put. The layout of the document itself, which may be completed in electronic or paper form, is equally straightforward, being divided, a little like the Ecogram, into metadata and dynamic data sections, as described below.

The Metadata section

The purpose of the metadata section is primarily that of organisation. This will become particularly pertinent as we progress upwards through the operational hierarchy.

The Type field

This denotes the effective level of the Summary Statement. It may be regional, national or international.

The Identifier field

This is the unique identifier for the Summary Statement. It is constructed of three, three letter codes to denote the region, country and international grouping. At the higher levels, the first codes may be replaced with zeros. For example, a unique identifier for the region of Saskatchewan might be SASCANNAM, while for Canada the identifier would be OOOCANNAM and for the North Americas it would be OOOOOONAM. The code for Northumberland in Britain would be NORGBREUR, while for Britain it would be OOOGBREUR and so on. This convention provides an intuitive way of quickly identifying the origins of a specific Summary Statement. This will become especially important once the methodology has been used for several years and the respective databases have become extensively populated populated.

The Year field

This is simply the year to which the Summary Statement appertains.

The Prepared by field

This should be the name of the individual who prepared the Summary Statement

Contact

This should be the primary contact information for the individual, typically in the form of an email address.

The Dynamic Data section

This section is where the summarised content is captured. It is divided into three logical sections as follows;

The Overview section

This is where a concise overview may be given which describes, in general terms, the situation observed at the level to which the Summary Statement refers. For example, at the regional level, it will be based upon the collection of Ecograms appertaining to that specific region and the inferences drawn from this detailed information. At the national level, it will pertain to the conclusions from the various regions within that country, and so on, leading to an international understanding that is particularly well informed. The preparer of the Summary Statement may of course enter as much, or as little information, as necessary to adequately describe the situation.

The Observed Trends section

This is a very important section where observed trends, both positive and negative may be captured together with their causes where properly understood. This information is very important and becomes increasingly so as we progress through the various operational levels. It is facilitated by the evolutionary information that we have observed, collected and interpreted over multiple iterations of Ecograms and Summary Statements across broadly defined areas. Recognising and understanding these evolutionary trends is an important factor within the broader Evolutionary Conservation model. Such an understanding serves to inform much of what we do at the practical remediation level. Observed trends also provide something of an ongoing audit trail of both understanding and associated actions.

The Recommendations section

This is where, upon qualified reflection, the entity responsible for producing the Summary Statement (which may be a government agency or other institution) may make recommendations based upon the previous two sections and the wealth of Ecogram derived information which has served to inform them. As we progress through the operational hierarchy, these recommendations may be further distilled into policy where appropriate, followed hopefully by the instigation of related conservation initiatives. The broad visibility of these higher level summaries within the Evolutionary Conservation community, is a factor which itself serves to support the development of a global understanding and, it is hoped, a global strategy. In this context, we may appreciated the value of the interconnected model and associated methodology provided by the Evolutionary Conservation initiative.

Summary

In this chapter we have described the Summary Statement and its anticipated usage. The distinction between the Ecogram and the Summary Statement reflects, in some ways, the variation of entities typically involved in the broader conservation effort. At the local initiative or 'ground' level, we have conservation practitioners who may themselves have a variety of practical skills and may be more or less academically qualified in one or more related disciplines. As we progress upward through the operational hierarchy, these individuals will be increasingly mixed with others, such as government agency workers, decision makers and even policy makers, who may have less practical experience, but are skilled in managing the broader administration. Consequently, we need two sets of related, but slightly differently presented information. Certainly, we require the lower level observation and measurement which may be captured via the Ecogram mechanism, but we also need more succinct summaries which may be quickly absorbed and understood by those at higher levels. Similarly, the linguistic style utilised within these Summary Statements may be subtly different in order to reflect their purpose. The combination of the two approaches, especially when merged together (as shall be explained later) provides for an unparalleled level of understanding to be developed in a uniform manner across boundaries. This promotes the development of a significantly enhanced international understanding and is at the heart of the Evolutionary Conservation concept.

An associated benefit of this mechanism is the correlation of information which, when properly interpreted, can serve to inform an intelligent global strategy for the management of our natural world as we progress throughout the 21st century. Such a strategy should not be developed in isolation, or with reference to purely theoretical concepts of environmental science. It must be based upon a detailed and continual observation across as wide an area as possible. An observation which is, in itself, continually validated and qualified as it develops within and across the broader network. This ensures that any such conclusions leading into the strategy are based upon reality and not simply assumptions. This reality will be constantly evolving and our knowledge constantly developing in alignment and in sympathy with this natural evolution. The entire mechanism being dynamic and thus able to continually track reality and inform our strategic response accordingly.

In the previous chapter, we mentioned that the humble Ecogram was in fact an extremely powerful tool. The same may be claimed for the Summary Statement. Deceptively simple in its presentation and operation, it can nevertheless become an extremely powerful agent for change. It represents the observation, appreciation and correlation of a potentially vast amount of qualified information. Cogent of these realities, we can start to appreciate the real value of Evolutionary Conservation.

7. Scalability

Abstract

In this chapter, we shall examine the scalability aspects of using Evolutionary Conservation and how the model allows for this in practice via the provided tools. We shall start with an introduction to scalability in general, before moving on to examine the various levels of scalability facilitated by the use of the Evolutionary Conservation mechanism. We shall note how the increasingly rich understanding generated at increasing scales of operation may also filter back down to the local level via continuous feedback, helping to inform local decision making accordingly.

Having explored the primary levels of scalability, we shall discuss the level of detail provided for within the Ecogram and associated database, and how this provides for flexibility, while maintaining a uniform approach to the observation and recording of key parameters. We shall also discuss the importance of interpretation and how this may be incorporated into the scalable Evolutionary Conservation model.

Introduction

The Evolutionary Conservation model was conceived at the outset to be both conceptual and practical. While we can discuss all manner of interesting ideas and possibilities with regard to conservation, if our ideas cannot translate into practical activity, then we are no further ahead in real terms. Informed discussion and associated research must translate into action if we are to improve upon the broader situation. With this in mind, one of the intentions of the Evolutionary Conservation concept, was always to provide a practical, workable model with which interested parties could practice the idea. The model uses a simple and intuitive tool set, as discussed in the previous chapters, which facilitates observation and the recording of information in a structured and repeatable manner. Deliberately positioned to be simple and intuitive, these tools may be used by anyone with a fundamental understanding of the natural world, be they academic professors or lay people from an associated local community. Consequently, we have the genesis of a mechanism which may be utilised upon a very wide scale.

If we consider all of the conservation initiatives currently being enacted in a given country, we shall no doubt find that, while each is well intentioned, there is very little coordination between them. Furthermore, the scientific discipline being applied might be quite different from one initiative to another, as might the overall objectives. Some may be concerned with a single species. Some may be focusing on a particular habitat. Some may be taking a broader environmental view. Few, if any, will be understanding the complex web of relationships, interactions and dependencies between them. If we extrapolate this position to a continental scale, we shall undoubtedly find even less coordination between initiatives. Extrapolating further to an international scale serves to highlight the issue. And yet, our planet is one large interactive mechanism upon which those relationships and dependencies play a vital part. If we wish to care for and preserve our natural world, we must surely deliberate upon this broader scale and strive to understand this complex web of relationships, interactions and dependencies. It may transpire that the complexity is beyond our immediate comprehension, but we can develop our understanding via a systematic programme of observation and correlation, undertaken over a period of years.

Of course, this already happens to a degree and there is a wonderful body of research and practical work already undertaken. In addition, specific disciplines have been developed to an advanced stage of understanding in their own right. The issue is translating these pockets of expertise into a more generally operable programme for the common good. We cannot ignore the part that politics plays in such matters and, in some cases, informing political will, let alone policy or strategy, might become quite challenging. In any event, in order for a broader range of conservation activity to be supported, a more universal mechanism for observation, documentation and correlation must be provided and embraced with some enthusiasm. In this chapter, we shall discuss how the Evolutionary Conservation mechanism may be utilised in order to provide the scalability and correlation necessary for a more widespread and better coordinated conservation effort.

Regional Scale

It is perhaps at a local and regional scale where Evolutionary Conservation is most easily and readily practised. And yet, the results of this regional conservation activity are crucially important to the broader perspective enabled by the Evolutionary Conservation model. Those practising the concept at local scales may take comfort from understanding that they are simultaneously contributing to the greater knowledge. Furthermore, this greater body of knowledge will build, year on year, to something way beyond initial expectations. But it all starts at a local level. A single initiative may use the Ecogram tool to very good effect in order to properly observe and document a given habitat or ecological system. Even this very first usage of the methodology will prove extremely valuable, encouraging the conservation team to understand the evolutionary aspects of what is being observed, while providing a mechanism with which to capture well informed thoughts, conclusions and even predictions. As subsequent Ecograms are developed, year on year, for the same area, the local knowledge will be further refined and honed into a continuum of understanding. An evolutionary picture will slowly emerge which, up until then, would simply have been unavailable. If the scope of Evolutionary Conservation was limited to local initiatives, it would indeed represent a significant step forwards from an operational perspective. Fortunately, there is no such limitation of scope and, the broader the usage of the model, the more powerful it becomes, as we shall discover within this chapter.

Now let us imagine that neighbouring initiatives within the same region are simultaneously developing Ecograms for their particular habitats or ecosystems, themselves building an incremental body of knowledge and expertise, regardless of the diversity of experience and skills among the individuals involved. By sharing this Ecogram data, the neighbouring initiatives may begin to understand the complex relationships and dependencies which exist across their immediate boundaries. The combined knowledge is now becoming far greater than the sum of its parts. Furthermore, this broader knowledge will, in itself, be developing incrementally as each year passes and new Ecograms are produced. Previous conclusions may be qualified and predictions revised and more keenly focused, while simultaneously being aligned with specialist, localised expertise. At a regional level, an agreed regional coordinating agency will be sent copies of each local Ecogram and these will be subsumed into a regional database. The regional coordinating agency may now understand not only every local initiative in a far greater detail, but may combine this knowledge into a particularly rich, and ever developing regional understanding. This, in turn, may be captured and further discussed within the Summary Statements produced at every level above the local initiative. Over a period of just a few years, this regional understanding will quickly surpass anything that exists today. Each year, following the submissions of local Ecograms, a regional report will be generated which will articulate this broader regional perspective, complete with an understanding of relationships and dependencies which may usefully inform local initiatives, and yet which no single initiative would have been able to form. At this juncture, the Evolutionary Conservation concept will be producing extremely valuable results. Let us not forget that contributors to this regional view may include schools, universities, government agencies, local communities and others where appropriate. Consequently, even at this level, we shall be engaging in a level of knowledge sharing and coordination well beyond that which currently exists.

National Scale

We have demonstrated that, at a regional level, the Evolutionary Conservation model provides substantial benefits for the enlightenment and pursuance of practical conservation. Imagine that we now collate all of these regional views into a greater, national perspective. We shall now have generated an incomparably rich understanding of the broader, national ecology, built upon a solid and uniquely informed foundation. Every detail of every Ecogram would have fed into this greater understanding, and will continue to do so, year on year. The result will be a level of ecological understanding that simply does not exist today, anywhere in the world. This, in turn, may be used effectively to inform national policy and to coordinate ongoing initiatives within the national theatre and according to an intelligently conceived strategy. Furthermore, there are various ways in which this enhanced understanding may be shared and disseminated back to regional and local initiatives of every kind, thus informing and enhancing their own activities within a continuous feedback loop. An annual report may be published by the national coordinating agency, providing a synopsis of important developments which affect the national position. This will include information around relationships, interactions and dependencies, supported by the detailed observations from each region. An on-line portal might also be provided at the national level, containing the enriched knowledge base that the Evolutionary Conservation model provides for. As years pass, this uniquely informed body of work will systematically grow richer and more inclusive. In addition, specialist academic research may become better aligned with, or even triggered by, the reality exposed by this enhanced knowledge and prioritised accordingly. This, in turn, will ensure that our conservation activities become increasingly effective, as all concerned will have a common focus around which they may construct their particular initiatives.

This extrapolation of observed and qualified information from local to regional and on to a national level, in a uniform and consistent manner, provides for the systematic development of an informed national perspective, well beyond that which exists in most countries today. Furthermore, by opening out this mechanism to schools, academia and even local communities where appropriate, the information flowing into the appropriate agencies will ensure that this enriched understanding is quickly developed. Once established, it will continue to develop over time and our skills will develop in parallel, allowing us to better understand and predict far reaching situations. This, in turn, will serve to better inform individual projects and ensure that the implications of our actions are properly understood. With this knowledge it may transpire that, occasionally, what seemed like an obvious route to take, may in fact turn out to be completely inappropriate for reasons not foreseen locally, including perhaps the broader evolutionary pattern. Such factors will be informed by the Evolutionary Conservation model which, at the national level, will prove an extremely valuable approach. For the very first time, our conservation strategies will be evolving in harmony with natural evolution, not in a theoretical manner or according to some artificially created aesthetic, but in direct relation to what is actually occurring.

Global Scale

From the national level, we may progress to international coordination, possibly aligned with defined economic or political communities, and from there to continental levels, where a further enhanced understanding may be generated and, finally to the global level, where we can really start to appreciate and understand our world within a proper context. The ultimate value and, indeed, aspiration of Evolutionary Conservation, would be to operate at the international, continental and global scales. It may sound like an ambitious objective, but it is an objective which is surely attainable, if there is a will to do so. The potential benefits to all concerned would be tangible and quickly realised. It may start with just a handful of countries collaborating together and coordinating the completion of their national

Ecograms in order that they may be subsumed into the international model - a model which will, in turn, be shared with all those contributing countries. Think of it! Even upon a continental scale, the enriched perspective that will be developed shall enlighten every initiative at every level below the primary coordinating master node. The knowledge available to each local initiative will be more far reaching than they could ever have hoped for in isolation. Furthermore, this knowledge will incorporate an evolutionary understanding in addition to a better comprehension of interactions and dependencies radiating out to every level beyond their own boundaries. And this detailed knowledge will be available to everyone, enabling a qualified care of our world to a degree never before possible.

If we extrapolate this thinking from the international to the global level, then the possibility of a single, global coordinating agency arises. This entity could be an existing government agency within a host country, who accepts the responsibility for the global initiative. Alternatively, it could be an existing political alliance or even a newly established entity, expressly for the purpose, perhaps within an academic institution or similar. The duties of such an entity would actually be quite straightforward and would entail an annual effort of receiving and subsuming all nationally completed Ecograms into a single, global view which, in turn, would be distributed back to the contributing countries whose central agency would be responsible for internal distribution. The global coordinating agency would also be responsible for maintaining the Ecogram template, the associated classification and other Evolutionary Conservation tools, ensuring that current versions are properly distributed. The global agency shall also be responsible for general communication and may maintain an associated web site and other tools in this context. In fact, the whole task could easily be coordinated and managed by a very small team upon a part time basis. The author has a crystal clear idea of how this would operate in practice and would of course happily liaise with such an agency in order to establish the service.

If such a service existed today, imagine the benefits to the global conservation effort. For the first time, we would start to think of our beautiful world as the single, homogeneous planet which it undoubtedly is, together with all the complex relationships, interactions and dependencies which, together, constitute life on Earth. Every initiative would have this all embracing perspective at its fingertips, enabling it to make informed decisions within the broader context. In addition, there would be a vibrant environment of knowledge sharing for the common good, operating within a practical mechanism, accessible to all. A mechanism elegant in its simplicity and transparent across all boundaries, geographic, political or cultural. Now that would be something quite wonderful and surely worth aspiring to? Our world deserves no less. We have destroyed so many natural habitats and wreaked havoc upon so many species, not to mention the damage we have done to nature's complex interactivity and evolutionary trajectory. It is surely time for us to recognise that we need something more than well intentioned, isolated initiatives operating within a local context. We must find a way of developing our broader understanding. An understanding of the complex interactions at every level and how these layers themselves interact, each one a product of the combined ecological minutiae within it. It is a daunting task, but a task which may nevertheless be managed, if we approach it in a systematic manner and within a spirit of true collaboration and coordination, as enabled by the Evolutionary Conservation model. If we establish this model now, each year will bring incremental gains to our combined understanding. An understanding that may be shared with everyone, from high level government agencies to the smallest and most remote local communities. An understanding to which all may contribute, from school students and amateur observers to established scientists. We shall have created an unparalleled environment of knowledge sharing in support of the most important challenge that faces civilisation. It is hoped therefore, that the concept of Evolutionary Conservation as described within these pages, strikes a chord in the hearts of those who care about our world and inspires them to adopt the model for use with their own conservation initiatives. It is further hoped that a suitable entity will be found to act as the global coordinator for this broader initiative. Time will tell whether such hopes are destined to be fulfilled.

Level of Detail

One factor affecting practical scalability lies in the level of detail captured at each level. If an attempt is made to capture too much detail, then the mechanism becomes unwieldy and not easily used by a broad cross section of users. Too little detail, and the mechanism becomes less effective, especially as it scales upward and this scalability is an important factor within the broader concept. Consequently, striking just the right balance is something of a challenge and this has been addressed within the Evolutionary Conservation model via a combination of standard, reusable classifications and free form textual description. The standard classification system brings uniformity to the recording of the fundamental factors associated with a given habitat or ecosystem. This allows for an easy comparison between sites, no matter where they are situated and, to a degree, irrespective of the mother language of the area concerned. Indeed, this methodology alone supports the systematic development of a broader understanding across boundaries as increasing numbers of sites are added. Furthermore, it is a system which is intuitive and straightforward in use for everyone concerned. The Ecogram template and classification list may be translated into any language using the Roman alphabet, without affecting the efficacy of the system, as the codes will remain common, allowing for ready comparison and the subsuming of datasets from one level to the next.

In addition to the Evolutionary Conservation classification system, much of the Ecogram is expressed as plain textual descriptions. International English is the preferred language for these entries and endeavours should be made to use English throughout the various layers. In instances where, perhaps at a local level, a different language is employed, then no doubt translations could be made at a higher level. Certainly, at the national level, all Ecograms expressed within the database should be in the English language. At any level, a non English speaker will at least be able to understand the classification codes and their meaning.

As time progresses, it may be that the classification system and, perhaps, the Ecogram template itself, is extended in order to accommodate a lower level of expression or perhaps other factors in order to cover a broader range of eventualities. As the mechanism is easily extensible, this would not be difficult. However, the communication of any such changes would need to permeate throughout the hierarchy and distribution of all users. This would be a task for the central coordination and administration team who, in turn, would be the only ones authorised to make such changes. A process will be established for requesting any such alterations.

Interpretation

One factor which cannot automatically be provided for is the interpretation of the data captured within the various Ecograms. Certainly, it is a simple matter to generate reports based upon certain classification items in order to ascertain similarities across areas and, indeed, this is provided for within the Evolutionary Conservation database which includes a variety of easy to use preformatted, parameterised reports. Similarly, the database tables may be accessed from other applications in order to import data into other specialised programmes for analytical purposes if required. However, the interpretation of Ecogram information, including the free form textual descriptions, must ultimately be aligned with scientific knowledge, experience and expertise at a variety of levels and across disciplines. This is facilitated by the amount and type of information gathered at each level. The free form fields within each Ecogram allow for this expertise to be exercised and expressed accordingly. As we progress through the various levels, different and complementary skills may be brought to bear, building upon the original observations and conclusions, and adding to those at every level. Consequently, we gain from both detailed local knowledge, specific regional understanding and more general national perspectives as Ecograms are systematically subsumed into higher levels. When this information is shared internationally, a further level of interpretation may be applied as the broader, international perspective is taken into consideration. When this is subsequently fed back down the chain to the regional and local levels, local practitioners may benefit from this broader interpretation, helping them to place their own endeavours into a better context. As time passes, the systematic updating and regeneration of this information provides for continual refinement, allowing for an increasingly better alignment of scientific understanding and practical reality. In addition, as all of this will be documented in a uniform manner, there will exist an effective audit trail, showing how things have developed over time. The Evolutionary Conservation model provides the mechanism to support this development of expertise and sharing of knowledge across boundaries. It also ensures that, as new understanding is developed outside of the Evolutionary Conservation initiative, perhaps within the realms of a specialised but related discipline, such an understanding may readily be aligned with, or even tested against, the reality as expressed within the Evolutionary Conservation hierarchy.

Summary

Within this chapter we have discussed the concept of scalability, acknowledging that scalability is at the heart of the Evolutionary Conservation model. The transition between local, regional and national levels provides for an increasingly broad comprehension to be developed and subsequently shared among all concerned. This continuous feedback loop is in itself a valuable factor for practical conservation, especially so as, year on year, the level of associated knowledge and understanding is systematically developed and enhanced. When this same model is extrapolated to an international framework of understanding, we have the potential to provide knowledge sharing upon an unprecedented scale and in a unified manner that all may contribute to. The resulting pool of information can provide important new insights into the complex relationships and dependencies within the natural world, informing our conservation initiatives accordingly. Ultimately, this same model may be extrapolated to a global scale, with the appointment of a central coordinating agency who would also be responsible for maintaining the Evolutionary Conservation model and associated tools. This infrastructure would provide the foundation upon which a remarkable level of understanding and expertise could be systematically developed. Herein lies the strength of a simple and intuitive model such as that described within these pages.

The level of detail required to support such a model is something which could no doubt be discussed at considerable length. The dichotomy is one between broad usability and scientific depth. The approach taken within the Evolutionary Conservation model is a combination of uniform simplicity and freedom of expression. On the one hand, much of the basic data is expressed via a standard, reusable classification system, while additional detail and interpretation may be captured via free form textual description. However, this freeform interpretation will be founded upon solid observation and uniform notation which may be readily understood across boundaries. Depending on the method of capture at the local level, a good deal of input to the Ecogram may be further simplified. If, for example, the source data is captured on a portable computer, then data may be entered directly into the Evolutionary Conservation database, in which case, data entry is simplified via intuitive drop down lists for all the standard fields and simple text editors for the free form fields. Alternatively, information may be captured in the field on paper, using the provided templates, and subsequently entered into the database. In any event, the model provides for a comprehensive level of detail to be captured where required, while remaining intuitive in use.

Interpretation of the captured data is equally important of course and this is another area where the Evolutionary Conservation model can prove extremely valuable as the system scales upward. At each level, additional expertise may be applied in order to more comprehensively interpret and understand the captured data. As Ecograms are subsumed and compared at successively higher levels, additional insights may be realised as a result of correlation. The enriched interpretation may then be fed back to the local level. This may happen at each level as the methodology scales upwards. Furthermore, there is scope to incorporate knowledge gained in independent research, validating it against the rich source of properly observed data that the model provides. In conclusion, this chapter has illustrated the scalability of the Evolutionary Conservation model, the associated benefits and why it has been conceived in this manner.

8. Sustainability

Abstract

In this chapter we shall stress the importance of sustainability with respect to conservation initiatives at every scale. We shall explain why this is considered important and how we cannot expect habitats or ecosystems to remain locked in time. Natural evolutionary processes are discussed in order to highlight the distinction between the natural world and conservation as often practised in a more static manner. We explain how and why the Ecogram model supports the concept of sustainability before concluding with a reinforcement of the need for sustainability with respect to everything we do under the broader banner of conservation. We shall also consider the consequences of failure regarding the establishment of a sustainable approach to conservation as described. This is necessarily a short chapter, but it covers an important factor which we should take fully into consideration within the broader subject.

Introduction

Within this work, we have variously made the distinction between conservation attempting to preserve a snapshot in time and the concept of Evolutionary Conservation which provides for a much more flexible approach, in a better alignment with the natural world. This distinction is particularly important with regard to the longer term sustainability of our conservation initiatives. In order to be sustainable, such initiatives must also be flexible and able to respond to changing conditions, ensuring that the right decisions are made at the right time. It may transpire that the observations made at the start of a given initiative become increasingly out of step with the ongoing reality and that, consequently, our conservation plan may also need to be revised. The Evolutionary Conservation model provides the necessary data with which to inform such decisions.

By maintaining this flexibility of approach over time, coupled to an intelligent appraisal at the start of a given project, we may ensure that our efforts remain both effective and sustainable. This infers regular review points as the initiative develops and an ongoing effort to monitor the habitat or ecosystem concerned into the future. This is how it should be. Our conservation initiatives should not be seen as a 'fit and forget' project, but rather as a sustained activity into the future for every habitat and ecosystem. In short, we should be constantly monitoring our world, to a fine level of detail and in a uniform manner across boundaries, in order to understand exactly what is occurring and why this should be the case. It is only with such knowledge that we can develop intelligent conservation strategies.

But how exactly do we define sustainability? As a situation or status capable of enduring? Perhaps it is not so much endurance for the sake of endurance, but the manner in which the situation may endure. In which case, we must have clearly defined objectives in the form of situations or states which we believe should endure for the common good, including situations which are themselves flexible and subject to constant change, as indeed, natural habitats are. Measuring the reality against these aspirations as time passes, provides us with a sense of sustainability. Informed observation lies at the heart of this analysis, and this must be undertaken upon a scale sufficient to uncover the myriad relationships and dependencies inherent in the natural world. The Evolutionary Conservation model supports just such an analysis. Furthermore, it provides the consistency of approach that renders this analysis in a uniform manner over time. Thus, we may derive a reasoned view of sustainability across a wide range of conservation initiatives, both in isolation and when grouped together. Furthermore, in a similar manner we may enhance our understanding of what is not sustainable and why.

Evolution

Evolution is nature's way of providing sustainability. By continual adjustment and a process of natural selection, a balance may be maintained within and across habitats and ecosystems. Indeed, if we hold that our world is one interconnected organism, then evolution is the key to the sustainability of life on Earth. Species and ecosystems exist within a process of constant adaptation and ongoing refinement. Habitats which existed many millions of years ago have changed over time, to a greater or lesser extent, depending upon a variety of factors. Consequently, the species which they are able to support have changed and, indeed the changed species do themselves affect, and are part of, the habitat or ecosystem concerned. Some species are able to endure in a relatively unchanged state, if their operational conditions are equally unchanged. Others are able to adapt into quite different forms, in alignment with their changing operational conditions. Yet more find themselves unable to adapt fast enough, or are otherwise out-competed and driven into extinction. And yet, the broader habitat or ecosystem is sustained. This is nature's way of providing a continuum. Albeit one which is constantly changing in its detail.

Such an arrangement might have endured well enough into the present time period, if it wasn't for the veritable swarming of the human race. As a species, we are having an unprecedented impact upon the world, due to our numbers and the manner in which we change our immediate environment. Natural processes, which may or may not have been in a gradual state of change, are suddenly interrupted by the impact of mankind and our alteration of the world around us. Some species are able to adapt to these rapid changes, while others will simply not be able to. Perhaps the most serious facet of this impact is habitat destruction. It has consequences far beyond the boundaries of any single actuality. The connections between habitats are often crucially important, not just for the associated species, but for the wellbeing of the global evolutionary model and the interactions between the geosphere, atmosphere, hydrosphere and biosphere, the whole of which defines our world.

Nature's evolutionary processes will ensure that, while the conditions remain viable, reaction and adaptation will continue to take place. The question is what form will these responses take? The more extreme the damage wreaked by the human species, the more extreme might be the response. Our comprehension of these complex natural processes is not sufficiently formed to be able to accurately predict such an extreme response. We simply have no conception of the true impact of our actions upon this established evolutionary process. The best we might manage is to mitigate the effects of this impact as far as is possible, via our various conservation initiatives, in order to avoid potential extremes of reaction. However, just as nature works upon a broad scale and across time, we must also incorporate these spatial and temporal factors into our plans if they are to prove sustainable. Natural evolution works at every level, from micro habitats and ecosystems, to the continental and oceanic scale, to the ultimate global scale. The combination of these activities provides the overall balance. The interaction between them provides for evolution and sustainability. In a similar manner, we must strive to understand these complexities of scale and interaction within our conservation initiatives, from the singular, through regional and continental, to global. It is only through this greater vision that we may find a workable balance. Developing and enabling this greater vision is the aspiration of Evolutionary Conservation.

It follows then, that in order to manage our conservation efforts in a sustainable manner, we must understand, and work in sympathy with, natural evolution. We must become expert at noting evolutionary change upon every scale, as well as understanding relationships and dependencies. We must become equally adept at maintaining a flexibility of approach which enables us to align with the changes we observe in a timely manner, even if this occasionally runs contrary to our original expectations. The Earth is a dynamic mechanism. We must be equally dynamic in our efforts to safeguard its precious resources and natural environments. It seems therefore that sustainability requires constant adjustment and associated action, understood and applied in an evolutionary manner. Indeed, except within the context of evolution, conservation is meaningless.

The Ecogram model

The Ecogram provides for a sustainable approach to conservation. It allows for the capture of a comprehensive set of information appertaining to a given habitat or ecosystem, in a uniform manner. It also provides an evolutionary snapshot by recording information for the present time, plus that for ten years and twenty five years in the past, and also to predict ten years and twenty five years into the future, as well as logging concerns for various factors. Furthermore, as the Ecogram is designed to be completed annually for every habitat, this perspective is updated, year on year, providing an increasingly enhanced appreciation, both of the habitat or ecosystem concerned and, importantly, of the evolutionary change affecting the area. Consequently, predictions will also become increasingly refined and more accurate. This enhanced knowledge informs decisions with respect to local conservation initiatives, ensuring that they may be managed into the future in a sustainable manner and is sympathy with natural processes. We are, in fact, providing sustainability via continual adaptation, thus echoing the natural evolutionary model to some degree.

We have previously explained how the Evolutionary Conservation model is scalable, from local initiatives, through regional, national and international perspectives and, ultimately, towards a common global perspective. This scalability is highly relevant to the concept of sustainability. For a given initiative to be sustainable, its understanding must extend beyond its own boundaries. It must have an understanding of all the external factors which might affect or otherwise contribute to its wellbeing. This includes relationships and interactions across boundaries, dependencies on other ecosystems, migrating or visiting species, developing species and other such variables. Understanding how these variables change over time is key to understanding the ongoing requirements for the host habitat or ecosystem. This, in turn, informs and supports the development of a sustainable conservation strategy. The scalable nature of the Ecogram model and its associated databases, supports this multiple feedback mechanism and may therefore be used to good effect to inform sustainable strategies. The more widely used the mechanism, the stronger our understanding will become in this context.

Users of the Evolutionary Conservation model will no doubt become adept at interpreting information, both via their own Ecograms and from those higher in the hierarchy when information is fed back to them, either directly or in the form of annual reports. As the Evolutionary Conservation network grows, this source of information will become increasingly rich in both its detail and the insights it provides. As local level Ecograms are refined and added back into the broader system, the understanding becomes further enhanced, year by year and at every level. Our ability to make correct decisions and develop an ongoing, sustainable strategy, should grow in proportion to this increasingly enhanced understanding. In short, the Evolutionary Conservation mechanisms, including the Ecogram, the classification system, the Summary Statements and the associated network of databases, provides significant support for the development of sustainable conservation strategies. Furthermore, this support is relevant at all levels, from the smallest local initiative to the international, continental and global scale.

Conclusion

There is a tendency for conservation initiatives to be finite projects, funded and orchestrated for a set period of time and with an agreed set of objectives (not all of which are actually to do with conservation). However, such an approach is not well aligned with the reality of the natural world. Natural habitats and ecosystems do not stand still in time. They are constantly evolving and adapting according to their particular constitution of species, relationships, interactions, dependencies and external influence. A conservation plan which may have looked reasonable at one point in time, may become quite out of step with the reality of the situation just a few years later. Consequently, conservation should not be thought of as a set of distinct projects undertaken at particular points in time, but rather as a continuous activity across wide scales. Everything we do should be designed to be sustainable into the future and, therefore, needs managing into the future. Furthermore, sustainability itself does not work in isolation. To be truly sustainable, a given habitat or ecosystem must be cognisant of its neighbouring habitats and the influence that they exert upon it, and vice versa. We must start to build that rich tapestry of understanding across boundaries in order to be able to take a broader, longer term view and translate that view into sustainable policies and actions. In order to bring that about, we need mechanisms for collaboration which also scale across boundaries of space and time. This is precisely what the Evolutionary Conservation model provides.

However, having an available model and establishing the necessary coordination and collaboration from a practical perspective are two different things. There must exist a will to move forwards with such a model and to use the information derived from it effectively. This will likely take some time to evolve into a fully working international framework, but it will evolve, so long as we use the methodology in support of local initiatives and start to subsume the resultant Ecograms into positions further up the hierarchy. We must simply have the courage to take that first step and start using the methodology. Of course, it isn't a perfect answer to everything, but it does provide us with a way forwards based upon intelligence, which is itself flexible and sustainable.

We can move the mountain by carrying away small stones and, as more of us are employed in stone carrying, so shall the task be achieved more quickly. However, we must pick up that first stone. The need to do so is becoming particularly pertinent as we progress into the 21st century. At least, the 21st century of what we consider to be civilised human existence. But how civilised is a civilisation that destroys the world around it, even though it understands the longer term consequences of doing so? How civilised is a world that is driven purely by greed? How civilised is a world without compassion for nature? We have been paying lip service to conservation for long enough. It is time that we really embraced the concept and placed it within a proper, global perspective. Given the rate of change on Earth and, especially, the rate of human proliferation, it may be that time is not on our side. If we could look ahead just five hundred years (no time at all in a geological sense) what would we discover? A decimated natural world within which we struggle for our very existence? A balanced and managed world wherein we have learned to maintain natural processes? Or something else? Some would hold that we shall not be here at all. Others, that we shall be here but that life on Earth will have become an artificial nightmare. Whatever the position, it is likely that our actions over the next few decades will have a dramatic influence upon it. Viewed in this light, the sooner we start to acknowledge sustainability with regard to our natural world, the better. To achieve such a level of sustainability, we must review and revise our approach to conservation. The concept of Evolutionary Conservation is providing a ray of hope in this respect, with a philosophy and associated mechanism that can transport us to where we should be. Shall we embrace it?

Summary

This has been a short chapter in order to stress the importance of sustainability within our conservation thinking and associated initiatives. We have suggested that conservation should not be seen as a method to preserve a given habitat as a snapshot in time, according to our view of how that habitat should appear and that, instead, we should strive to understand the natural evolutionary dynamics and work within them. We stressed that, in the natural world, a given habitat or ecosystem is indeed a constantly evolving entity, with a complex pattern of inter-dependencies and relationships which serve to define its course along the evolutionary path. This includes the particular assemblage of species to be found at any point along this path. Consequently, it is unrealistic to believe that we can somehow fix this position in time and space. We must take a more flexible approach and work with nature, rather than contrary to its natural course.

We explained how the Ecogram mechanism supports such a way of working, incrementally helping to build and strengthen our knowledge of the evolutionary dynamics, not just in relation to a single initiative, but across initiatives. This, in itself, is an important factor with respect to sustainability, as our enhanced knowledge will spread across boundaries of geography, politics and culture, helping us to understand relationships and dependencies and, as a result, develop better policies and conservation action plans. This, in turn, will ensure that our various initiatives are both more sustainable and more cost effective. Indeed, the mechanism itself may be considered sustainable due to its inherent scalability and extendibility, both of which were original design objectives. Those who embrace this model will find that it supports their own sustainable strategy via its simple repeatability and ease of use. If we fail to develop a coordinated approach as described within this volume, we shall miss the opportunity to establish such a sustainable model and may well be overtaken by events. We simply must understand the position that we are now facing and what this means for the continuance of civilisation.

9. A Practical Methodology

Abstract

In this chapter we shall turn our attention to practical matters. Specifically, what is required to practice the Evolutionary Conservation concept and produce valuable results from it. We shall discuss how a variety of skills, experience and human resource might usefully be engaged within the broader preparation of the Ecogram. Practical observation, measurement and testing are similarly discussed and placed into an appropriate context, before moving on to the process of recording information and preparing the finished Ecogram. We shall then discuss the broader management of Ecograms within a defined administrative structure at various levels, from the local to global. This discussion will place the Evolutionary Conservation initiative into a practical, workable context, highlighting the enormous value that may be derived from its intelligent execution.

Introduction

In order to work in a consistent manner and in alignment with a given methodology, such as the Evolutionary Conservation model, we must understand both the mechanisms involved and the requirements for working with it. Ensuring that these requirements can be met should form part of the preparation for working with the methodology. There may also be a necessity to incorporate existing ways of working into the broader methodology and, if need be, documenting the process accordingly. As with many endeavours, the way in which we work can have a significant effect upon the work itself and the quality of its outputs. With respect to conservation, this is particularly important as the effect may have lasting implications. It is important therefore to create a suitable working structure and process which is compatible with the chosen methodology and practically operable over time.

If the chosen methodology is scalable, as is the case with Evolutionary Conservation, then consideration must be given to the structure of the organisation or agency undertaking the conservation initiative. If it is a government agency, then it should be a straightforward matter to establish a logical hierarchy from national to regional and on to local, ensuring that the necessary requirements are in place at each level which, in most cases, will already be the case. If a separate organisation, then it may be possible to feed into an existing national structure, or establish a similar, parallel structure which, ultimately, feeds into the highest available level. This participant architecture will evolve naturally over time and, in the case of Evolutionary Conservation, may be overseen by a central administration. While this evolution is taking place, participants will still enjoy the benefits of using the methodology at whatever levels they are connected to or, in isolated cases, even in connection with a single conservation initiative. Participating agencies should therefore be thinking ahead and planning accordingly, preferably via a well conceived and properly managed project with clearly identified milestones towards the end objective. In such a manner we may realise the potential of adherence to a defined methodology. But it needs to be a well considered and well planned exercise. In addition, it needs to be properly communicated to all concerned. It follows then, that preparing to use the methodology and ensuring that an operable architecture is in place is crucially important to its overall success. From there, there are other factors to take into consideration, as discussed throughout this chapter.

Resources and skills

Having the right resources, skills and, in some cases, equipment in place is clearly important. However, this does not necessarily mean that everyone involved should be a qualified specialist. Indeed, much good work may be undertaken by those who are at the start of their career, as well as lay enthusiasts. Harnessing this enthusiasm and readily available resource would be extremely valuable from the broader community perspective. For example, sixth form school students represent a wonderful resource, distributed throughout the world which, with a little encouragement and guidance, can undertake observational tasks upon a scale that eludes qualified specialists. Those studying related subjects at universities may similarly be employed in observation within their particular locales and surrounding areas. Even enthusiastic members of local communities may make valuable contributions in this context. Indeed, the history of science is peppered with examples of unqualified enthusiasts contributing significantly to our understanding across a number of disciplines. The same can happen for conservation. All of these people may be usefully engaged in a detailed and systematic programme of observation, guided by the methodology itself.

As these observations are collected, better qualified individuals may scrutinise them and, where appropriate, add their own observations and conclusions. This may occur at every level as completed Ecograms get passed upwards through the hierarchy and Summary Statements produced accordingly. As these documents are completed year by year, local experience and associated competence will be enhanced accordingly, this knowledge being easily transferred among individuals. In different regions, these skills will adopt a slightly different complexion according to the local ecology, providing a level of overall expertise that could not be matched by that of a single focus. Consequently, this distributed and open approach to participation in a larger initiative has many benefits, both from the accumulation of information perspective and for overall educational purposes.

In parallel, we shall of course be developing specialist skills within our universities, in the Earth and environmental sciences, biology, botany and related areas, leading to properly qualified individuals who may be deployed as experts across a number of initiatives. However there will not be sufficient numbers of these individuals to be engaged in every project in every area and so, complementing their ranks by the inclusion of non-graduated students and local enthusiasts can ensure that we gather valuable information from a much broader base. This, in turn, places us in a much better position to understand the broader perspective, including the myriad relationships and dependencies across habitats and ecosystems, as documented by our core of observers. As Ecogram information is subsumed into the higher levels, specialists may analyse the data in a number of ways in order to develop this broader understanding, comfortable in the knowledge that the data have been collected in a consistent and uniform manner, regardless of location. This is part of the value that a defined methodology such as Evolutionary Conservation can bring to our broader understanding of ecological issues.

In terms of actual training, the tools and materials made available via the Evolutionary Conservation initiative may complement, and bring a new dimension to, formal teaching methods in related subjects at a variety of levels. Indeed, they will be of particular value with respect to the transition from classroom theory to practical field work and the analysis of associated observations. This will help to reinforce understanding among students and, hopefully, to further fuel their enthusiasm for the subject. As the broader initiative develops, additional materials may be made available in this context.

Observation

Observation may be considered an acquired skill, or even an art. Some are naturally observant and notice the fine detail of all around them, others are less so, but may be trained to notice pertinent factors. Some may take an organised and methodical approach, using transects and various instruments, while others take an intuitive random approach. Somewhere among these variations is an optimal approach to observation which may prove practically valuable in the gathering of pertinent information with which to populate the Ecogram.

Precisely what observations are made will no doubt depend upon the situation at hand and what the associated objectives are. However, one may generalise to some degree. The Ecogram does itself guide the observer towards important criteria and, when completed in its entirety, will ensure that a comprehensive view of the habitat or ecosystem concerned is captured. Beyond the Ecogram, one might engage in a finer level of observation for specific areas of interest. In general, it will often be pertinent to observe at both the macro and micro levels, but especially at the micro level. We should look for the smaller details which might easily go unnoticed. A subtle change in the lower level detail might be an indicator of things to come, in either a positive or negative sense. We should also look for the absence of familiar species as well as the presence of the unfamiliar, both in the static sense and for visiting species, and of course for indications of invasive species. Choosing a resident indicator species and noting any change over time will be valuable and the Ecogram provides for this, as it does for noting soil acidity and other parameters.

The Ecogram and associated classification allows for a broad range of observation to be undertaken within a variety of natural habitats. If there are substantial areas where other factors are reliably noted, then it is perfectly possible to extend the classification to accommodate these factors. However, this should only ever be undertaken by the central administrative function and subsequently made available to all. There should only ever be one version of the classification in use at a given time, otherwise much confusion could arise when harmonising Ecograms which have used different parameters within their observation and documentation.

Measurement and testing

Having observed relevant details, and especially changes, we should categorise and, where appropriate, measure these details in order to accurately record them. The Ecogram provides for the broader categorisation as well as, via free form text entry, detailed measurements where necessary. Some factors, such as soil acidity for example, have a standardised measurement (pH values) while others might conceivably use different methods for linear measurement or weight. The Evolutionary Conservation initiative recommends the European decimal system and standard scientific notation for all such measurements.

Practitioners should ensure that they have the proper tools for the job to hand. A tool kit of basic measuring devices and equipment necessary for testing certain conditions should be established and properly maintained. Such a tool kit may easily be shared by small groups of individuals where appropriate and should be checked after every field trip. More sophisticated equipment, as might be used for laboratory analysis for example, might be kept safely at a base location where practitioners may gather after a field trip. This may include the appropriate Evolutionary Conservation database.

Information recording

Taking measurements and recording observations in the field can be difficult under some conditions, such as extreme weather conditions or areas of challenging topography. Safety should be a prime consideration in this respect, as should any potential interference or damage to natural habitats. Common parameters such as temperature, humidity, wind speed and direction, soil acidity, water level, area and so on may easily be measured using the appropriate instruments. Other factors, such as observed change, species diversity, unusual conditions and developments may best be noted in free form textual descriptions and diagrams. For capturing such information, the humble paper pad and pencil is probably the best tool, together with a large, clear plastic bag which may shelter the pad against the elements when necessary. With practice, the observer will quickly develop a reliable method of capturing pertinent information.

The camera can also be an invaluable aide to recording information in the field. However, care should be taken as to what information is captured photographically, at what scale, and in support of what other information. Generally, photographs are useful in depicting overall landscape or habitat features for reference purposes. This may be especially useful for recording change, by taking photographs each year in exactly the same position and at a variety of scales. Photography may also be useful to record small scale features, perhaps in relation to indicator species for example. However, care should be exercised in order to ensure correct colour balance, control over geometric distortion and so on. This will generally entail the use of good quality equipment, together with an appropriate level of applied skill and consistency of approach. Nevertheless, a good quality, properly managed photographic archive can be an invaluable aid to conservation within a given area and should be considered accordingly.

Ecogram preparation

Typically, information will be gathered in the field in a number of ways in order to populate the final Ecogram for a given area. There may be several individuals, or teams of individuals, dedicated to researching different aspects within the broader scenario. Some of these may be trained observers, some may be specialist practitioners in a particular field, and some may simply be enthusiasts contributing to the broader initiative. Consequently, among the collected data, there will no doubt be some variance of approach and the relative level of detail captured. This is to be expected and is perfectly acceptable for our purposes. Once the information has been collected, a single individual (in each area) should be appointed with the responsibility for collating the information and entering it into the Ecogram. This individual may then liaise with other team members as necessary to confirm any unclear details among the data.

If coordinated as recommended above, the individual responsible for populating and submitting the Ecogram may choose how best to accomplish this task. For example, they might choose to maintain the Ecogram as an electronic document (using the template supplied) that may easily be edited and revised on a continual basis throughout the data gathering period, before finally entering the data into the local copy of the Evolutionary Conservation database. Alternatively, they may prefer to enter the information directly into the database as the data gathering process continues. Each data record may of course be edited and updated at will.

There may be other factors to consider, such as the requirement for specialist knowledge where the interpretation of an observed condition proves problematic. Such factors should be anticipated and allowed for in time to complete the Ecogram. If members of the observation team are non English speakers, then time must also be taken for language normalisation, although this may be a minimal requirement, depending upon the extent of free form notes. The primary task however, will simply be to coordinate the activities of observers throughout the information gathering phase and to ensure that every component of the Ecogram is fully provided for. When all is complete, the final task will be to enter the information into the local Evolutionary Conservation database. This will ordinarily be a straightforward exercise which should not be too time consuming. Entering the code based data will be quickly undertaken due to the drop down lists within the user interface of the database software. For free form text entry, this may be undertaken manually or, where appropriate, existing files, perhaps prepared by key observers, may simply be imported via the integral word processor. There is ample scope to make notes about any aspect of the habitat or ecosystem under consideration. In addition, for ongoing local use, relevant material may be added to the repository in support of ongoing analysis. This may include externally produced scientific papers, notes about processes and procedures, and other material as appropriate.

Preparing and producing the Ecogram should be an annual event. In this way, we may observe and track changes as well as note the efficacy of our ongoing conservation efforts. Over time, this approach provides the evolutionary information which is often missing from single point conservation initiatives. Furthermore, such a methodology supports the ongoing development of local expertise and understanding, ensuring that our conservation efforts are increasingly aligned with the reality of the natural world. Indeed, as Ecograms are produced and entered into the local database, year on year, we shall be developing an increasingly rich body of work to document this ongoing understanding, making it available to future researchers while systematically increasing its pertinence.

Ecogram management

Having perfected the processes around the establishment of local Ecograms and the local database, we may turn our attention towards participation in the broader Evolutionary Conservation initiative. Within a given country, this infers the acceptance of the concept at a national level, probably under the auspices of a relevant government agency. At this national level, a catalogue of regions may be developed, each one reporting back to the central national administration. Within each region, a catalogue of local initiatives will be maintained, each one reporting back to the regional administration. As each Ecogram is completed at the local level, this is forwarded to the regional administration. When all local Ecograms are completed, the regional administration forwards these on to the national administration, together with its own notes and conclusions. At the central, national administration level, we will now have an unprecedented level of understanding for that particular year, based upon solid observation and measurement across a broad spectrum of related initiatives.

Let us now extrapolate the model from national to international. If international centres are established, each one with a defined set of countries falling under its umbrella, as might happen at a continental level, or perhaps in association with a defined economic community for example, then we shall similarly establish an enhanced level of understanding at this international level. Ecograms, Summary Statements, notes and conclusions may all be subsumed at this level in order to develop this rich tapestry of knowledge and associated understanding of our world.

Ultimately, it would be possible, and desirable, to take this to the ultimate, global level. In this context, a global Evolutionary Conservation authority would be established, whose purpose would be not only to collate all of the international information and produce a detailed annual report, but also to manage the Evolutionary Conservation mechanism and its broader administration. It will consequently provide a central focus for information and advice, without deterring or necessarily interfering with national administration. It would however make sensible recommendations if it observed differences of approach which might be detrimental to the broader, global perspective.

As we may readily appreciate from this model, the humble Ecogram, Summary Statement and other tools provide a common foundation upon which an invaluable and unique understanding may systematically be developed. The management of the Ecogram, once properly completed, is an integral part of this model and must be given due consideration accordingly. If orchestrated as described, a quite wonderful web of understanding may quickly be developed, especially if we engage as many as possible in the uniform creation of Ecograms at the local level. This is important as, from the broader conservation perspective, time may not be on our side. It is similarly important therefore that, at each administrative level, a proper ongoing operational plan is developed and rigidly enacted. Good organisation lies at the heart of any such endeavour.

Summary

In this section, we have discussed and described that which is necessary to establish and maintain a practical methodology. The emphasis here is on the concept of practicality. Developing an overly complex methodology, however scientifically sound, would ultimately prove of little practical value if it could not be used universally. A key objective of Evolutionary Conservation is that the methodology should easily be used by everybody and that the derived knowledge should be equally easily shared and made available to all. To achieve such an objective, we need a defined structure of both working methodology and associated administration. The Evolutionary Conservation tool set provides for the working methodology and the associated administration simply needs to be defined and agreed before adopting the methodology. Once this structure is in place, even at a regional and national level, the Evolutionary Conservation concept will very quickly produce valuable results.

Naturally, we need to understand the level of practical skill and experience required to properly complete an Ecogram, based upon observation which, in fact, may be undertaken at a variety of skill levels, thus engaging a far greater number of individuals within the broader initiative. We have discussed how this might work in practice, placing an emphasis upon observation and measurement. In reality, a mixture of skills and experience may be brought to bear within any given initiative. This, in turn, is a valuable aid to education as young students may be introduced to the natural sciences and practical conservation via local conservation initiatives, thus gaining valuable practical experience to complement their curricular studies. In a similar vein, local community members may also be engaged, often bringing invaluable local knowledge into the broader picture accordingly. The completion of Summary Statements adds another level of interpretation where experienced scientists and administrators can produce inferences from the supplied Ecogram data and set these out logically in representation of the areas concerned.

We have discussed the practicality of information recording and subsequent Ecogram and Summary Statement preparation. It is important that such activities are undertaken according to a strict timetable in order to ensure the annual preparation of information at every level. This leads us to the broader Ecogram management and the necessity of establishing a practical, hierarchical structure of administration, including feed forward and feed back loops to ensure knowledge sharing and the creation of a broader understanding for the common good. We have consequently described this in some detail.

In short, a practical methodology has been provided via the Evolutionary Conservation initiative and the associated tools. The success of the concept will be proportional to the degree with which we embrace and practice the methodology. If adopted enthusiastically, invaluable enhancements to our broader understanding may be quickly realised. The Evolutionary Conservation concept is, in fact, the golden thread with which our rich and beautiful tapestry of understanding may be woven. However, we must have the will to do so and the necessary organisation and practical orchestration of effort. It is entirely realisable.

10. Tools

Abstract

In this section, we shall briefly acknowledge the documentary tools explained previously before moving on to describe the Evolutionary Conservation database and its operation. We shall do so via a selection of screen shots from the actual database, explaining the purpose and functionality of each as we progress through the application in a logical manner. This will provide the reader with a good understanding of the database tool, while reinforcing the underlying premise of the Evolutionary Conservation concept. We shall also discuss the distributed database model, its practical operation, and how it supports a variety of associated activities such as knowledge sharing and policy formation.

Introduction

A new concept such as Evolutionary Conservation is easily discussed in theory, even down to quite a low abstraction of detail. However, in order to become practical, it must be associated with a methodology, and such a methodology will ordinarily be accompanied by a set of basic tools with which to practice it. This, in turn, introduces a defined rigour together with a uniformity of approach which renders the methodology both scalable and sustainable. We have already discussed the desirability of these traits and have similarly introduced the primary tools. These include:

The Ecogram

The primary vehicle for collecting information following observation and measurement and which includes provision to capture conclusions, perceived threats and suggested actions in a free form manner.

The Classification System

The classification system provides a logical catalogue of codes which represent certain environmental or biological factors and conditions. The use of these codes provides consistency across boundaries and enables correlation and comparison accordingly. Furthermore, from a data management perspective, this approach facilitates analysis in a variety of ways.

The Summary Statement

The Summary Statement provides a higher level of abstraction from the Ecogram at successive levels above the base, local level. This provides for subsequent interpretation and, where necessary, for specialist skills to be brought in as the broader ecological picture is developed. It also provides for a systematically enhanced perspective to be developed as Summary Statements are absorbed throughout the hierarchy towards the final, global level.

The combination of these three documentary instruments allows for a given habitat or ecosystem to be properly defined and, importantly, to be placed within an increasingly broader context. Furthermore, the Ecogram additionally provides for an evolutionary context to be incorporated into the broader understanding, an understanding which is scalable in both the temporal and spatial domains. We may thus construct an increasingly rich tapestry of related knowledge and share this knowledge across boundaries for the common good using these tools. This is one of the cornerstones of the Evolutionary Conservation approach. There is an additional requirement however, to devise a system whereby all such information may be both archived and made readily available, wherever it is needed. In addition, the system should facilitate interpretation at each level, feed back and feed forward capabilities and, ultimately, for overall annual reports to be created. The mechanism should also be intuitive and easily used at all levels. This requirement is met by the Evolutionary Conservation database, as discussed in the next section.

The Database

In order to provide a distributed database model, one must provide compatibility between databases at the various different operational levels. The functionality required at levels above the local level differs slightly as one progresses through the operational hierarchy. However, much of this difference resides in matters of administration and scientific interpretation. The decision was therefore taken to design a single database model which could be used at all levels. This is a practical approach as it ensures there is but one database architecture to be maintained and distributed among users accordingly. If, for specific reasons of their own, a particular administration wishes to use additional tools within the analysis of Evolutionary Conservation data, this is perfectly possible as the underlying database tables are in the popular dBase format, allowing them to easily be read by a variety of applications. This was also a conscious decision, as was the approach of using only text based fields. Consequently, we have a single database model, providing high levels of functionality while remaining intuitive in use, based upon an underlying database architecture which lends itself to other purposes. However, if an administration wishes to analyse data outside of the database (which, in the majority of cases will never be necessary) then it is strongly advised to copy the relevant tables to another location before using them. The supplied database is designed for Microsoft Windows operating systems and should run on all versions from Windows 2000 onwards. The various database sections and associated screens will now be discussed, although users will learn quickly enough through practical experience.

Figure 10.1. The Evolutionary Conservation database start up screen

A small welcome screen is the first thing that users will see when starting the database. This provides confirmation that all is well and that the database has been correctly installed and is functioning normally.

Having initiated the software application, clicking on the Continue button will take the user to the operational section of the database. This is where Ecogram data may be entered, including information appertaining to perceived risks, recommended actions and conclusions. This is undertaken via a tabbed dialogue which is explained below.

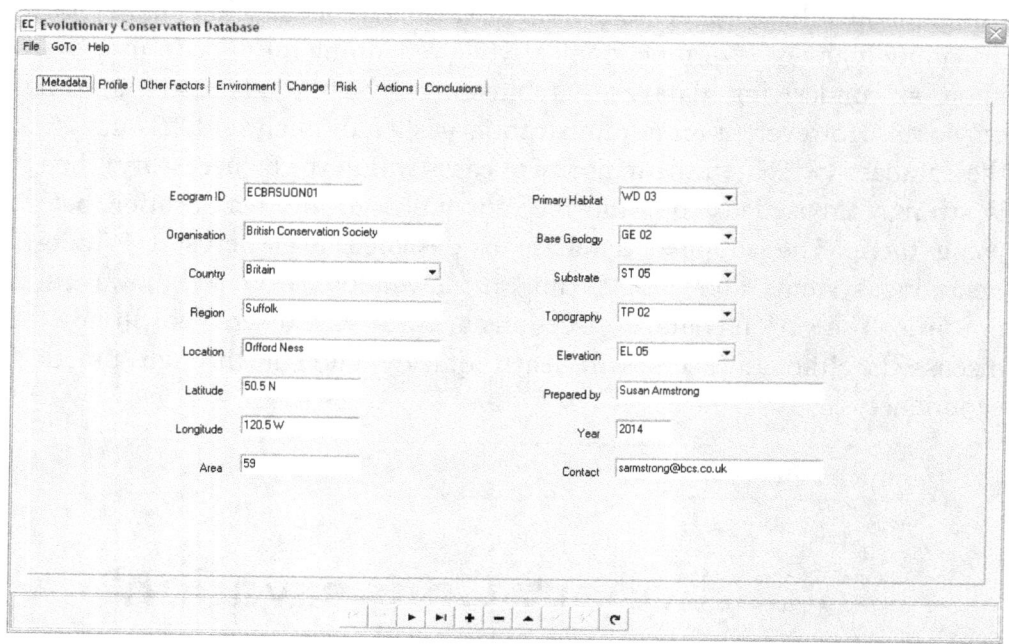

Figure 10.2 The Metadata section of the main database

The first tab is where the metadata appertaining to this particular Ecogram is entered. The fields on the left hand side are self explanatory and, following a unique identifier according to convention, consist of geographic information which places the habitat or ecosystem concerned in a precise location. The fields on the right hand side provide some fundamental information about that particular location, such as primary habitat, base geology, substrate, topography and elevation. This allows for Ecograms to be quickly correlated or compared for various purposes. Lastly, we have details of who prepared the Ecogram, their contact details and the year. Several of the fields feature drop down dialogue boxes, enabling the user to quickly select information in a standard format, thus providing both expediency and consistency across Ecograms. This section provides a good set of basic information with which to describe a given situation before moving on to greater levels of detail. We may now move along the tabbed dialogue from left to right in order to complete subsequent sections, the next of which is the Profile tab.

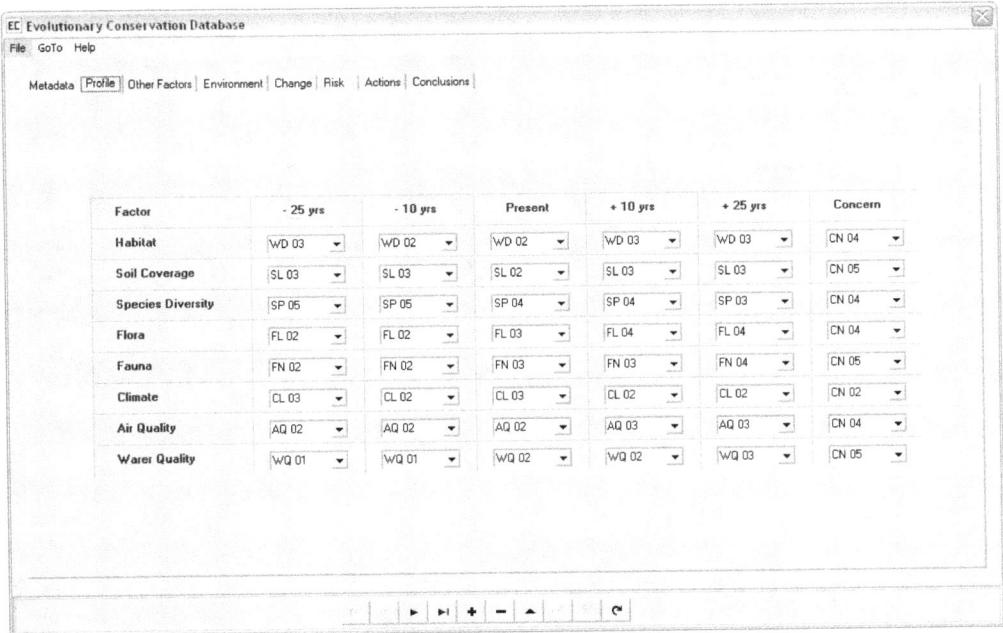

Figure 10.3 The Profile section of the main database.

The Profile section is particularly important as it is here that the current status of the habitat or ecosystem concerned is captured, together with past information and predictions for the future. This provides for an evolutionary perspective which, over a period of years, will become increasingly refined, providing a sound base upon which to form conclusions and plan ahead accordingly. Completing this section is straightforward as all field information is selected from drop down dialogues which display the classification codes and their meaning. There is, in fact, a significant amount of information displayed on this single screen, which can tell the practised eye a good deal about the habitat or ecosystem to which it pertains, including evolutionary trends, may readily be deduced from this displayed information.

If the database and classification were later to be translated into different languages, the codes will remain the same, maintaining consistency as data is subsumed into higher levels within the Evolutionary Conservation hierarchy. The next section along the tabbed dialogue provides scope for capturing additional factors.

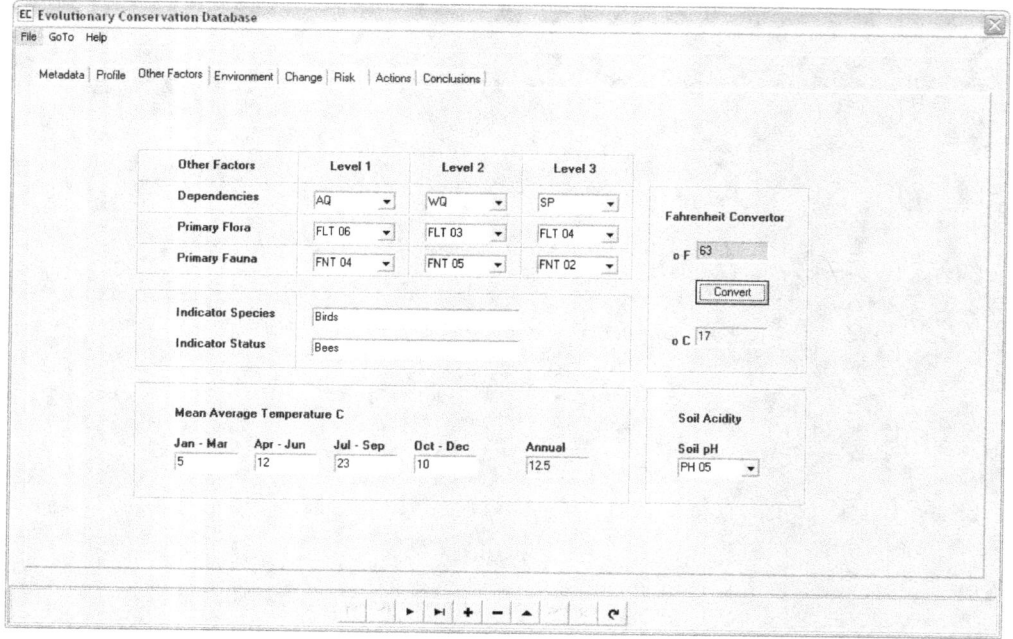

Figure 10.4 The Other Factors screen

This section complements the main data with the provision to capture information about known dependencies, the primary flora species and the primary fauna species, at three different levels, providing a useful snapshot from a species and dependencies perspective. There is also provision to designate an indicator species and to record the status of that species for this particular year. Over time, the indicator species status will provide a useful audit trail of how the habitat or ecosystem is actually evolving. There is also provision on this screen to capture mean average temperature per quarter and this is automatically averaged for the year by the database system. Lastly, soil acidity may also be noted here and, for many areas, this will be an important ongoing measure. Usability and simplicity of presentation endures throughout these different screens, an important consideration for non habituated users. We may now move on to the Environment tab.

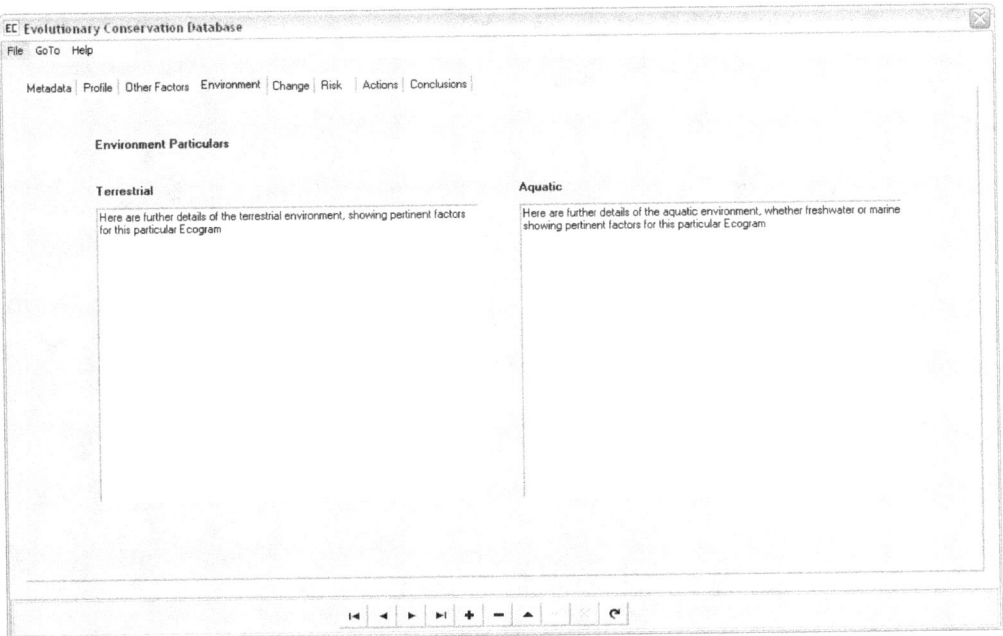

Figure 10.5 The Environment section

Actually, we have already captured a good deal of specific environmental information within the preceding screens. However, much of this has been coded and, in this section, we have the opportunity to enter free form text in order to describe both terrestrial and aquatic environments within our particular habitat or ecosystem, at a greater level of detail. One may enter text directly into the boxes displayed on this screen. Alternatively, by right clicking within either box, the Evolutionary Conservation text editor may be displayed. This is a lightweight word processor which, in addition to providing comprehensive formatting functionality, allows for existing documents to be imported or for text in these sections to be exported. This may be useful for instances where reports may be created separately and simply imported into the database. This may be the case when separate team members, or even departments, are preparing general reports appertaining to a specific area. It was deemed important to provide this flexibility within the Evolutionary Conservation database, as the data it contains may be used in a variety of ways at different stages within specific projects.. Now we may continue to the Change section.

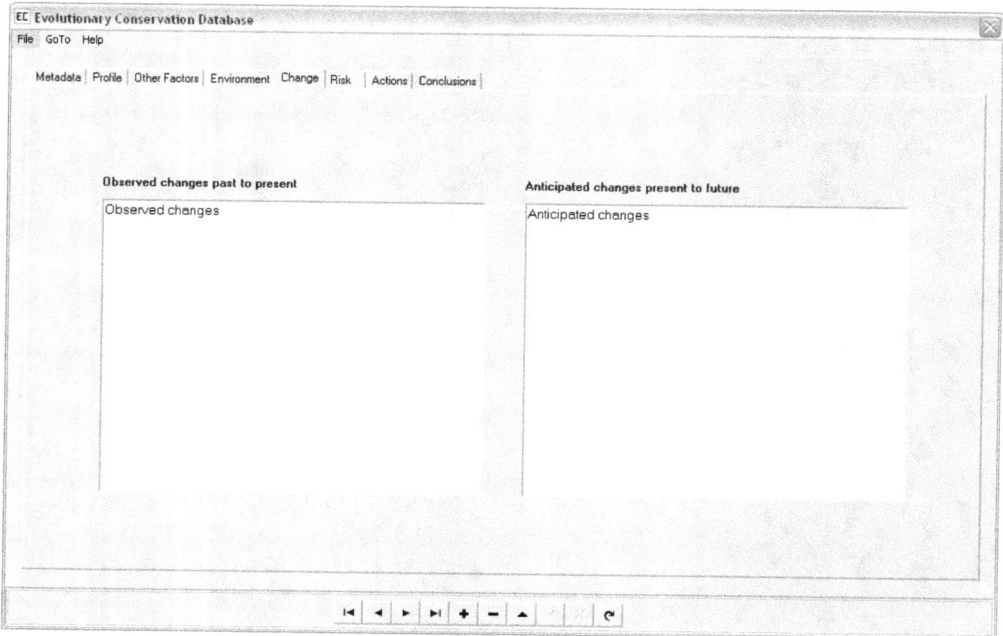

Figure 10.6 The Change section.

This section is divided into two: changes observed from the past to the present time and changes anticipated from the present time into the future. Once Ecograms have been produced for a number of years in relation to a particular area, the past to present changes may be captured with a very high degree of accuracy, focusing upon areas of particular concern. Similarly, the prediction of future changes based upon a combination of previous history and existing expertise will become increasingly accurate, supporting the development of meaningful conservation policies and strategies for the area concerned. As in the previous screen, text may be entered directly into the displayed boxes, or via the integral Evolutionary Conservation text editor. The next section appertains to perceived risk.

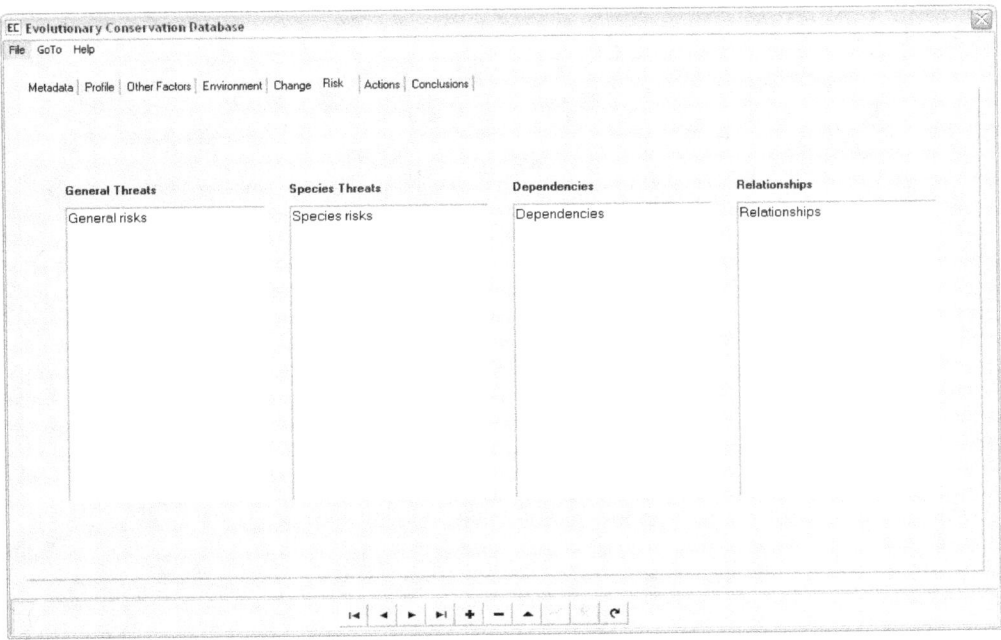

Figure 10.7 The Risk section.

This section is where we may capture all information concerning perceived risks within the habitat or ecosystem being monitored. It is divided into four sub sections. The first deals with general threats and may capture an overall synopsis of the current situation. The second deals specifically with species threats and is where we may list all species perceived to be under threat and prioritise them accordingly. The third section describes dependencies, between species, habitats and in more general terms, and is, in fact, a very important component within the Ecogram. The fourth section captures relationships which, in some cases, may become quite complex. The combination of these factors provides for a comprehensive appreciation of the risks associated with a given area. Over time, this section will become increasingly important as, year by year, the information is further validated and enhanced. Once again, information may be entered directly or imported from other documents. Having comprehensively described the general situation within this and the previous screens, we may now turn our attention towards required actions.

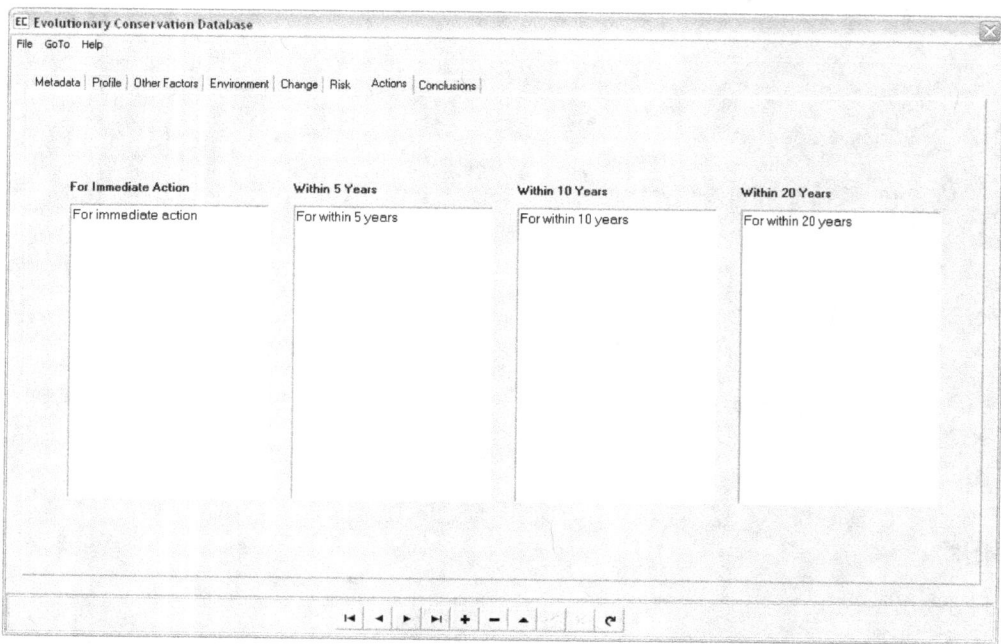

Figure 10.8 The Actions section

The Actions section is an important area where we may capture proposed remedial actions in support of our conservation efforts. Over time, this will provide an invaluable audit trail depicting the evolution of the habitat or ecosystem under consideration, in direct relation to our activities. The Actions section is divided into items for immediate action and items for action within five, ten and twenty years, thus providing a proper ongoing plan. This section may be refined within successive Ecograms, validating current activities and reviewing and fine tuning the future plan accordingly. As in other sections, information may be imported from related documentation if required, using the text editor.

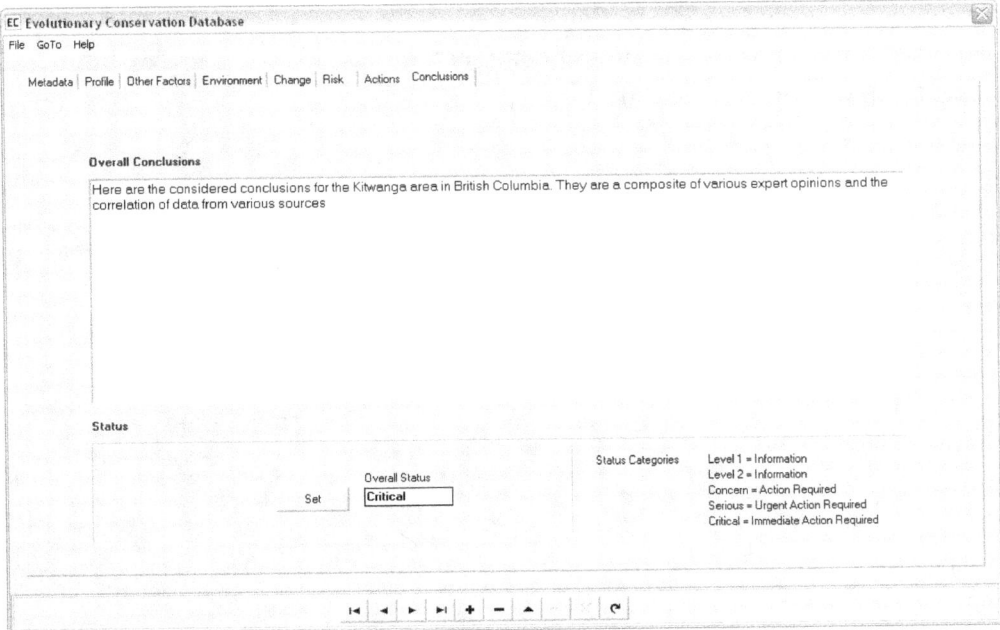

Figure 10.9 The Conclusions section

The final screen within the main Ecogram area of the database is where we may capture our conclusions appertaining to this year's Ecogram. It may be that we wish to import a separately created report into this section, or create the conclusions report right here and export it as a separate document. In any event, this is an important part of every Ecogram. In addition to the free form textual description entered here, there is displayed an Overall Status factor. This is created automatically, based upon information entered within other sections where the standard classifications are used. This provides for a simple way of comparing the status of multiple Ecograms and, if required, grouping them according to criticality. The Reports section of the database will cover this aspect in greater detail.

The database sections concerned with the direct capture of Ecogram data provide a wealth of information appertaining to a specific habitat or ecosystem. Furthermore, this intelligence is refined and strengthened over time, leading to a firm and accurate foundation upon which associated policies may be developed and decisions taken accordingly. One may start to appreciate the potential power and hence value of the Evolutionary Conservation concept when using the provided database tool. However, there is more to the database than just capturing Ecogram information and it can usefully become the focus and coordinating force of conservation activities at every level in which it is used. A facility which is particularly useful in this context is the reports section, where a series of standard reports may easily be generated.

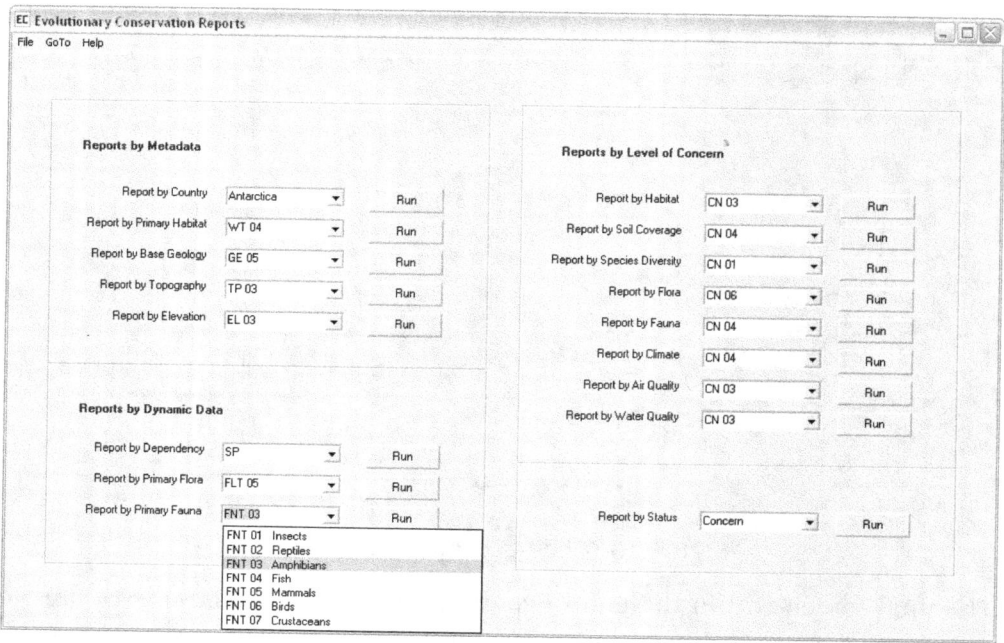

Figure 10.10 The Reports section of the database.

The Reports section provides for a number of preformatted reports to easily be created with just a couple of button clicks. The available reports are logically grouped into areas of metadata, dynamic data and levels of concern, while a separate report focuses upon status. Adjacent to each report description on the screen is a drop down dialogue box, allowing the selection of a parameter against which to generate and run the report. For example, for Report by Country, the parameter is the country and, for Report by Primary Habitat, the parameter is the primary habitat, and so on. Clicking on the Run button (after a parameter has been selected) runs a parameterised query against the data set and uses the output to generate a report. This report is then automatically formatted and previewed on screen, from where it may be viewed, printed or saved as a file for future analysis. This provides for a simple to use, consistent reporting mechanism that may be employed at every level, from local to global. It is represents an efficient way of asking questions about the dataset held at each level.

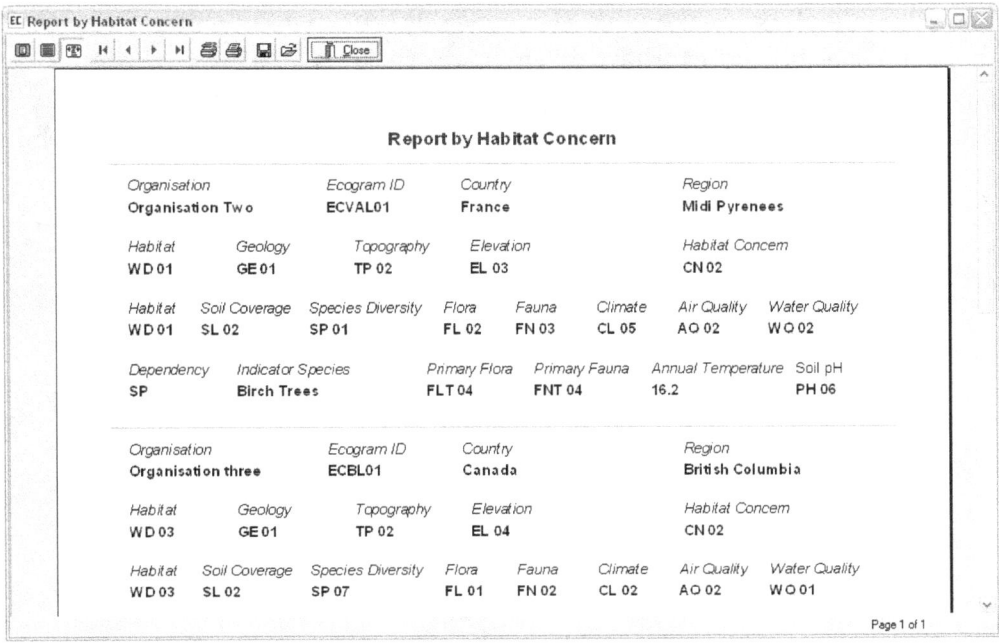

Figure 10.11 An example report

In the above figure an example report, in this case Report by Habitat Concern, is shown. The report is divided into records, each depicting the salient fields appertaining to such a report. If there are multiple pages for the report, the user may simply navigate among them using the controls at the top of the form. From here, they may also adjust the viewing scale, setup a printer and print the report or save the report to a file for subsequent analysis. They may also open a previously saved report from this form. The reporting engine is an integral part of the Evolutionary Conservation database and will no doubt fulfil the requirements of the majority of users. If however users wished to use a separate reporting tool against the data held within the main database, this would be perfectly possible. The database tables are of a standard dBase format and are easily viewed by a broad range of applications. However, users wishing to do so, should make a backup copy of the main database first and then use the reporting tool of their choice against this backed up copy. This will ensure that use of a proprietary reporting tool does not corrupt the Evolutionary Conservation database. Whatever approach is taken, reports provide a way of extracting pertinent information which may then be used to inform higher level annual reports, to support discussions and to feed into policies and ongoing operational strategies.

As with any database, one must also consider the day to day management of the database and efforts have been made to keep this task as simple as possible, so as not to require any specialist database administration skills. A separate screen provides a direct view on to the main database table while also providing for some basic administration tasks.

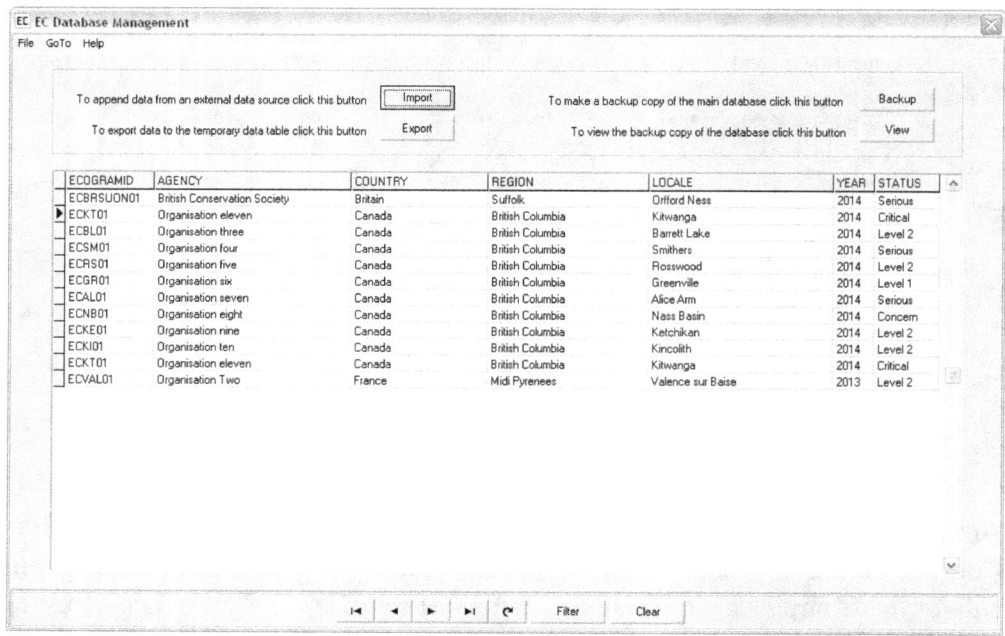

Figure 10.12 The Database Management or DB Admin screen

The Database Management screen provides some important functionality. Firstly, it provides a direct view onto the main database table. This view deliberately has a restricted field list as, with over ninety fields in the main table, it would otherwise prove unwieldy. In any event, its purpose is simply to provide an overview of the records within the database. The fields displayed include the Ecogram ID, the agency concerned, the country, region and locale, the year to which the Ecogram pertains and the Ecogram status. This synopsis will be all that is needed to view, identify and understand a particular Ecogram record.

In the top section of the screen a group of buttons provide fundamental management features as follows. The Import button allows for a dataset provided by a lower level entity within the Evolutionary Conservation hierarchy to be imported into this database. Specific instructions are provided within the database help file as to how to accomplish this task. The database compares the two datasets and any records found in the guest dataset that are not present within the host dataset will automatically be imported.

The Export button is used to create a dataset which may subsequently be sent to a higher entity within the Evolutionary Conservation hierarchy for importation into their database. It creates a table of existing records in the correct format and this table may simply be sent to the correct entity, either by electronic mail or other mechanism. The receiving entity places this table in their database folder and uses the Import button to add the records to the host database.

The Backup button, as the name suggests, simply creates a backup copy of the main database for security purposes. If a backup copy already exists, this will be overwritten with the new data, ensuring that the last taken backup is always available. Below this button is the View button which simply allows for the backed up data to be viewed, confirming that the backup has been successfully undertaken. Clicking on this button displays a separate screen so as not to be confused with the main administration section.

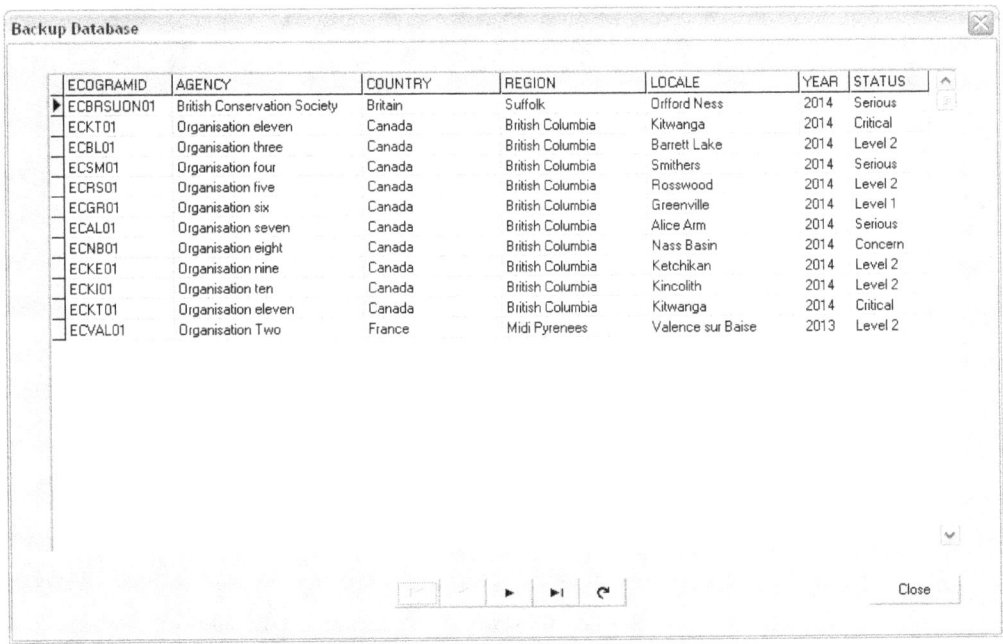

Figure 10.13 The view onto the backed up database

The backup database view simply shows the records within the backed up database table, using the same fields that are visible within the main

Database Administration screen. The user may easily navigate among these records using the controls provided. This is a modal screen which requires the user to close it before any other operations may be undertaken.

The Evolutionary Conservation model also allows for annual Summary Statements to be produced in support of the Ecogram. These statements have several uses. Firstly, they provide a useful mechanism for summarising the primary factors revealed within the Ecogram in a manner which may easily be understood by non professionals. In addition, they provide for a mechanism which may be used separately in order to assist the formation of policy or to provide national and international reports. While succinct in themselves, each one is associated directly with its supporting Ecogram, providing lower levels of extrapolation where necessary. Naturally, the Evolutionary Conservation database has provision to store these summary statements and to navigate among them. This is facilitated by a separate database table which may be viewed from the Summary Statement Database screen.

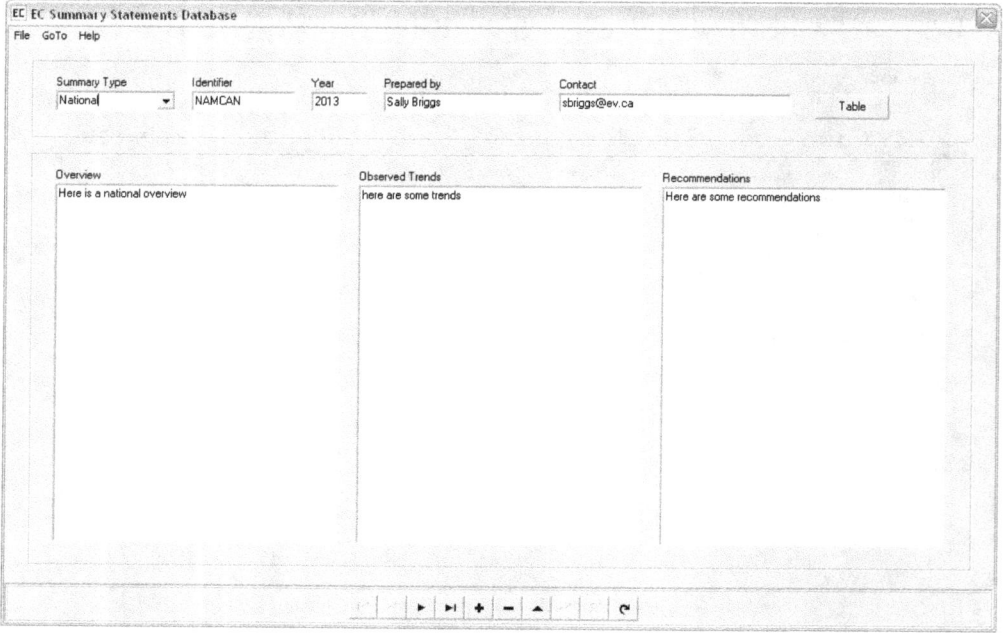

Figure 10.14 The Summary Statement Database

The Summary Statement Database is quite straightforward and includes fields to identify the statement level (such as regional, national or international), the year and creator, and of course a unique identifier. Free form text fields provide for an overview of the general situation, a summary of observed trends and associated recommendations. As with the main database, information may be entered directly or via the Evolutionary Conservation text editor, from where external documents may also be imported. The navigation controls allow individual records to be added, edited or selected. Many users, when not actually entering information, may prefer to see a list of all the available summary statements. This is easily facilitated by clicking on the Table button within the top section of the screen, which displays a separate form for this purpose.

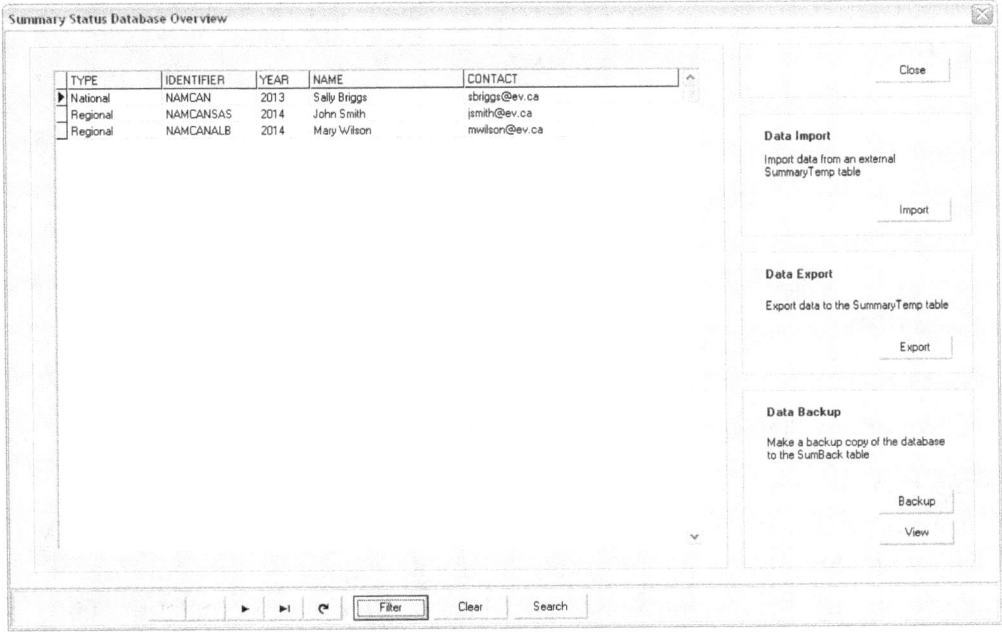

Figure 10.15 The Summary Status Database Overview screen

This screen, while appearing deceptively simple, actually provides for some powerful functionality. The main window simply supplies a list of all the available summary statements, showing their type, their unique identifier, the year to which they pertain and their creator. Selecting a summary statement within this list and returning to the main Summary Statement database will display the selected statement in full detail. This in itself is quite useful. However, there are several additional features. The same facilities for Import, Export and data Backup that exist within the main database are also available here, and they work in exactly the same way and therefore need no further explanation. The associated controls are all present on the right hand side of the screen. At the bottom of the screen, in addition to the primary database navigation controls, are three additional buttons marked Filter, Clear and Search. These provide for additional manipulation of the database table and are explained below.

The Filter button displays a dialogue which enables filtering of the dataset by various criteria.

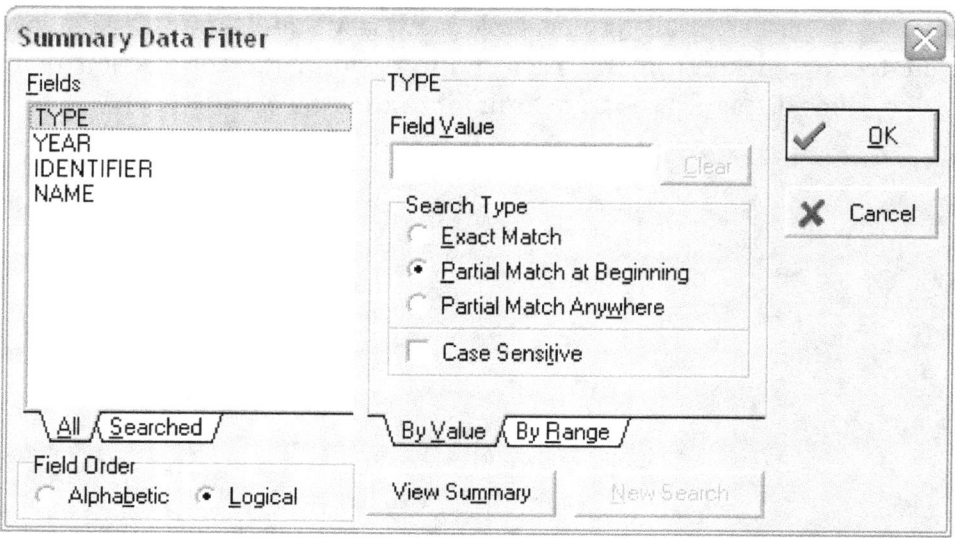

Figure 10.16 The Summary Data Filter dialogue

From this dialogue the user may select any field upon which to apply a filter. For example, selecting the year field and entering a field value of '2014' will display all the records appertaining to the year 2014. When entering filter criteria in the field value box, it is also possible to instruct the filter to operate on an exact match basis, a partial match at the beginning of the entered string or a partial match anywhere. This provides for a high degree of flexibility when searching for specific information. Alternatively, clicking on the By Range tab allows for a range of values to be entered. For example, we could have entered between 2012 and 2014 as filter criteria against the year field. Having entered the desired criteria, clicking on the OK button will apply the filter to the dataset and only those records matching the criteria will be displayed.

The Clear button at the bottom of the Summary Statements database screen simply clears the in place filter and shows all the records within the dataset. It performs the same function as the Clear button within the filter dialogue.

Sometimes of course, one might wish simply to search for some very specific information within the dataset, in which case, a simpler approach could be taken. This is provided for by clicking on the Search button at the bottom of the form.

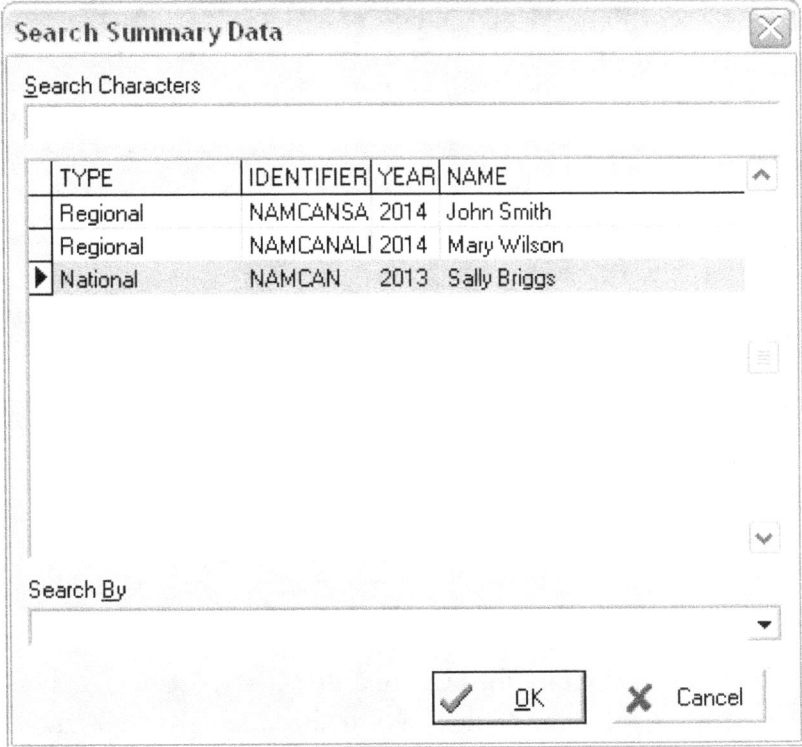

Figure 10.17 The Search dialogue

The Search dialogue allows for the selection of a field to search against via the drop down box at the bottom of the screen. Having done so, entering search criteria in the box at the top of the screen will find the first record in the dataset that complies with the search criteria. It will start the search as characters are entered and will therefore work quite quickly in relation to most datasets. Clicking on the OK button will return the user to the main Summary Statement database and the selected record will be displayed automatically.

There is another section within the Evolutionary Conservation database which provides a repository where associated information may be stored. This might be in the form of external scientific papers of special interest, guidance documents for conservation practitioners, the documentation of local procedures, or any other information that might be useful to the teams operating at the level where the database is being employed. This is a very useful and easily used feature, accessed from the main GoTo menu.

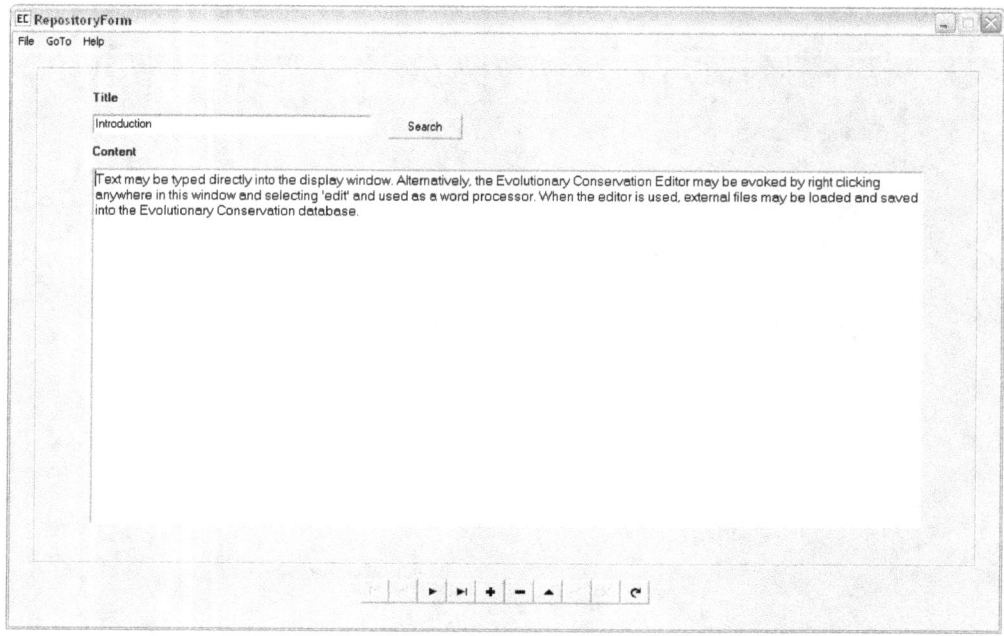

Figure 10.18 The Repository database

Text may be entered directly into the text box if required, and then given a descriptive title within the Title field before being saved as a record. Alternatively, existing documents may be imported by right clicking in the text box and displaying the Evolutionary Conservation text editor. Each document must be given a title in order to be able to search for it and display it when required.

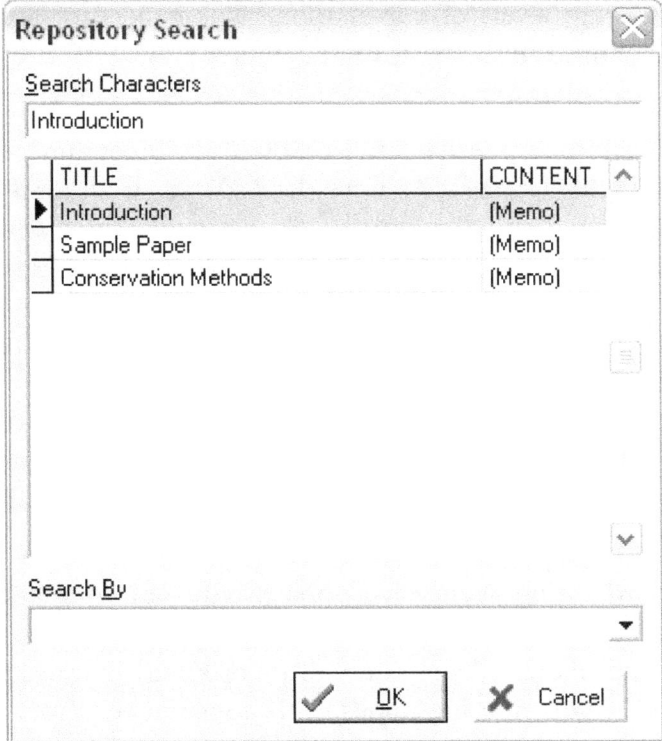

Figure 10.19 The Repository search function

A search facility is provided via the special dialogue which will quickly find a specific paper within the repository. Users might like to adopt their own naming convention in order to logically group documents together within the repository. It is anticipated that, in most cases, this will simply contain a handful of relevant documents, according to the operational level.

Within the database, there also exists an online help facility to guide users through the various screens and associated functionality.

The distributed database model

Within the previous section, we have described at some length the Evolutionary Conservation database and its functionality. It is important that practitioners understand this database as it functions as the key component within the broader, distributed information model, a model which itself lies at the heart of the Evolutionary Conservation concept. Within this model there exists a hierarchy of operational nodes, from local initiative through regional groups, national, international and, ultimately global. At each of these levels, the same database application may be used, albeit with differing levels of information. This makes for a simple, easily maintained technical infrastructure as there is just one application to distribute and maintain.

Every year, the local initiative will complete the Ecogram and enter this information into the database. At a pre-defined date, each local initiative will send its database table to the appropriate regional centre where it will be imported into the regional database. A regional summary statement will be produced and entered into the database at this level, before both of these database tables are sent to the national centre, where they will be subsumed into the national database and a national summary statement produced. This information will, in turn, be sent to the next international or continental level where, once again, the information will be subsumed into the international database and, finally, on to a global level where all information may be subsumed into a master database.

The global coordinating agency will then produce an annual report which may be sent back down the chain to all participating levels. Similarly, at international and national levels, annual reports may be produced and sent back down to the contributing nodes. This constant feed forward and feed back activity provides for an unprecedented level of knowledge sharing. Furthermore, the shared information will be based upon a combination of low level field observation and informed interpretation as data is passed up the hierarchy and then coordinated into broader observations, conclusions and qualified reports. All of this is facilitated by the single database model described within this chapter which is, in turn, informed by the original Ecogram documents and thus based upon observed reality..

The database tool that has initially been provided will meet all of these objectives and has an intuitive, easily used interface. However, as time passes, a more sophisticated model might be designed and built should it be deemed important to do so. The tool itself is of less importance than the underlying concept and operational methodology.

Summary

In this chapter, we have explored the tool set which underpins the Evolutionary Conservation concept. The emphasis has been on providing a straightforward, easily understood mechanism which may be employed at several levels of operational activity and used by a variety of practitioners. The fundamental mechanism of Ecogram, Classification and Summary

Statement provides the necessary documentation and introduces a uniform approach to the recording of related information. These tools in themselves provide everything necessary to practice the Evolutionary Conservation concept. However, the database acts as a unifying and coordinating mechanism where all such information may be brought together in a logical manner for subsequent analysis. Consequently, the database will no doubt become the central focus at all levels of activity. Furthermore, it provides an invaluable audit trail at all levels and this is important for the purposes of understanding evolutionary trends. In addition, the various reports available may be used for a variety of purposes at each level within the operational hierarchy, including training and education, knowledge sharing and to support the formation of associated policies.

With any new concept or proposed methodology, it is important to be able to translate the idea into practical, operational activity. To do so usually requires an aligned set of tools. However, it is equally important that these tools be intuitive in use and easily understood by a broad cross section of practitioners and administrators. This has been the goal for the tools described within this section.

11. A Framework of Understanding

Abstract

This is a short chapter which highlights the desirability of working within a defined framework of understanding. We shall describe why this is necessary and how it might be achieved at various levels, from national to international and beyond. We shall similarly describe how this may be achieved from a practical perspective, making use of the tools already provided within the Evolutionary Conservation model. We shall continue on to a discussion of how such ideas may be extrapolated into the future and the opportunities which may exist in this context. Throughout, the emphasis is on engagement and inclusive thinking in support of the common good. This in itself is an important tenet within the broader concept of Evolutionary Conservation which aims to be easily used by a wide cross section of practitioners, official agencies and communities.

Understanding the broader perspective

In previous chapters we have stressed the importance of understanding the broader perspective with respect to conservation in general. This is especially important due to the complex web of relationships, interactions and dependencies that exist within and between habitats and ecosystems. This is not just related to species, but to the inter operable environment in its entirety. Each area reacts and interacts with those around it, while the whole interacts in every dimension within this beautiful and complex tapestry of life upon Earth. Even disregarding the rich variety of species, our planet is alive with processes and activities which themselves have relationships and dependencies between the various spheres. Adding the layer of species, both flora and fauna, simply deepens this complex, interactive situation. Given this reality, it seems inappropriate to consider conservation within isolated boundaries of either time or space. Nature simply doesn't work in this way. It follows then, that the broader our understanding of the whole, the better we shall be able to understand what we observe at the local level and be able to apply intelligent reasoning accordingly.

Developing such an understanding will, in most cases, take time, especially if we are to understand the evolutionary component within the broader perspective. This in itself needs to be observed and correlated over time in order to understand what has happened in the past, what is happening currently and what might happen in the future. This perspective must then be juxtapositioned with an understanding of the relationships and dependencies among species within and beyond the particular habitat or ecosystem under consideration. This is not a small task and one could easily spend a lifetime studying a single habitat and still not fully comprehend the detail within it. In such cases, our understanding, such as it is, will often be overtaken by events as evolutionary effects take hold. Furthermore, this could happen upon a fairly wide scale if we pursue a myriad of individual, relatively isolated conservation initiatives, causing the overall picture to become increasingly complex.

In light of the above, a different approach might usefully be followed wherein we develop a better coordinated framework of shared understanding for the common good. In such a manner, we could usefully accelerate our combined understanding of the natural world and all that it contains, including the evolutionary processes to which it is subject. This shared understanding may then be applied to individual initiatives in a manner which renders them more relevant to the broader situation. To a very small extent, we have this already, as specialists in particular areas participate in conferences, publish their research and generally interact within the community. However, this remains a little fragmented due to departmental, operational and sometimes political boundaries. Examples of this can be seen by looking at individual nations where, quite often, one will find significantly different approaches being followed across state or provincial boundaries as well as between departments. This is unfortunate as, occasionally, best practice is simply not followed in a uniform manner. When we consider the international perspective, the issue is simply accentuated. And yet, as we have observed, nature knows no such boundaries. Consequently, if we are to be effective in our conservation endeavours, we need to develop this broader framework of understanding and uniformity of approach. This is the goal of Evolutionary Conservation, to promote and facilitate just such an understanding via the provision of a working methodology which may easily be used by all concerned, regardless of geography, politics or culture..

Working in harmony

To enable this greater understanding and ensure that the resulting knowledge is shared without prejudice, we require a model which allows us to work in a coordinated, harmonious manner while allowing for flexibility at the local level. This entails knowledge sharing, not only of the Ecogram and Summary Statement data for specific initiatives, but of our specialist skills and interpretations across scientific domains. This is facilitated by the structure of the Evolutionary Conservation mechanism which allows for specialist input at every layer of the operational hierarchy. Furthermore, the Summary Statements provide additional scope for informed comment to be appended at every level above the local initiative. When used wisely, this mechanism will facilitate an increasingly rich tapestry of understanding to be created as information is shared across spatial boundaries. In addition, this understanding will be further enriched over time as successive editions of Ecogram data become available, thus providing an evolutionary context.

All of this is perfectly possible and readily realisable via the provided mechanism. However, in order for it to work properly and reach its potential, it requires human input. Consequently, it is important to establish a clear structure within national boundaries, ensuring a coherent network that encompasses the central national administration, the regional offices and, within each region, the various local conservation initiatives. When such a network is in place, a country may enjoy the full benefit of the Evolutionary Conservation concept within its national boundaries. The organisation of this structure should ideally be undertaken by the relevant government agency who, in turn, may appoint the regional representatives, probably within the existing model of regional government, ensuring that the data flow is properly in place at each level, using the Evolutionary Conservation database as the primary focus at each operational node. Alternatively, it would be possible for a similar structure to be emplaced within the private sector, perhaps via a non-profit organisation working within this sphere of activity. Conceivably, both could be operable simultaneously if working on separate initiatives, with the overall data coordinated at official, national level. Similarly, in many countries, it may be possible to engage the education network, both secondary schools and universities, in order to further develop and utilise their skills in both observation and remediation. Tapping this huge reservoir of resource could make a significant difference to the efficacy of our conservation efforts and accelerate our understanding of the rich tapestry of our world, including evolutionary factors as they affect natural habitats and ecosystems.

However, in order to identify, engage with and harness such resources, there needs to be a suitable level of awareness with respect to the Evolutionary Conservation concept. It follows then, that a comprehensive communications exercise would also need to be undertaken within every participating country or state. There exist a variety of channels through which such communication may be made, many of them at little or no cost. These may include engagement with both the printed and broadcast media, various mechanisms on the Internet, existing channels in academia and government, local initiatives and many more. From a national perspective, one of the first steps, having established the technical and operational infrastructure, will be to design and mount a comprehensive and sustainable communications campaign. Naturally, such a campaign may also stress the need for conservation itself. In such a manner, a steadily growing infrastructure of human resource may be established.

Looking to the future

In order to look towards the future we must understand the past as well as current realities. We need top do this, not only from a conservation perspective, but from an administration and operational perspective. We must understand current deficiencies and limitations and develop a plan to resolve all such issues. This task may benefit from some adventurous thinking around the identification and engagement of the required resources, as well as communicating the broader requirement. We have already mentioned the fact that secondary schools and universities may be one source of enthusiastic and informed resource, especially if one considers the global position. With secondary schools especially, there exist a vast number of such entities situated in all corners of the world. They represent a wonderful source of potential observation with respect to our natural habitats and ecosystems. Their engagement in this context would accelerate our understanding of our world very considerably. There may be other sources, such as multi national industry for example, where dedicated and enthusiastic resources may be found. We need to think way beyond the boundaries of those existing bodies involved with conservation. This is entirely feasible. We just need some creative thinking coupled to a positive disposition. Given what is at stake, one would hope that such a task would not be beyond our powers of imagination and execution.

The wonderful thing about the potential of this idea is that, following some effort to initialise and establish the concept, it will, if properly administered, quickly assume a momentum of its own. In such a manner it might grow almost exponentially as increasing numbers of authorities and institutions come to understand its potential. If this were to be the case, and there is no reason why it should not be, then we would quickly find ourselves in the position of creating a considerably enhanced understanding of our world and how it is reacting to contemporary challenges. From such an understanding, we shall be in a much better position to develop intelligent strategies with which to manage our catalogue of conservation initiatives. The Evolutionary Conservation concept has provided the basis for an operational framework, together with an intuitive set of tools with which to realise the actuality of it. However, this alone is not sufficient. We also need the human involvement, with the necessary enthusiasm and commitment to make it work. There exist a very large number of government agencies, academic institutions, non profit organisations, multi national commercial entities and others, all of whom claim an interest in conservation and the well-being of our planet. The Evolutionary Conservation initiative provides them with the perfect opportunity to demonstrate both their commitment and integrity in this context. It is hoped that they will respond accordingly.

With the right level of engagement and enthusiastic management, the Evolutionary Conservation concept could very quickly be developed into a practical vehicle for the common good with respect to informed knowledge sharing, upon an unprecedented scale. As the mechanism develops, no doubt all manner of interesting ideas will surface as to how such knowledge may be applied to practical situations. Such ideas may be fed back into the system via the in place tools and infrastructure, ensuring that the model becomes increasingly pertinent as we progress into the future, with a common understanding which, year on year, becomes increasingly astute. This idea lies at the heart of Evolutionary Conservation. However, we have to start somewhere. Individual conservation initiatives must be encouraged to start using the Evolutionary Conservation mechanism as intended and to be ready to share their results. This is the first step from which something wonderful might develop. But we have to make that first step. If you are reading this and have a direct involvement with a conservation initiative, I therefore urge you to download the templates and tools from the Evolutionary Conservation web site and start using them within the context of that initiative. While it may seem a little strange at first, the value will quickly become self evident and the project will undoubtedly benefit as a result. But more importantly, you will be contributing to the greater effort, where every contribution has a valuable part to play within this broader framework of understanding. It may take us a little while to properly establish this framework, but it is entirely feasible to do so. Furthermore, what more noble or pertinent aspiration could we have in our 21st century world?

Summary

We have stressed the need to understand the broader perspective and to adapt our thinking around conservation to it. In particular, to understand the complex web of interactions and dependencies which characterise our diverse habitats and ecosystems. In order to accomplish this, we need to develop efficient ways of working together and to ensure that knowledge is shared, without prejudice, across geographic, political and cultural boundaries. This, in turn, requires a framework of understanding. A shared vision, within which conservation initiatives may be coordinated and knowledge shared at various levels, from the field operational level to the highest level of administration.

Tools are provided with which to orchestrate such a collaboration and yet, tools alone are not enough, we need an intelligent cooperation between entities, fuelled by this common vision. In this respect, the Evolutionary Conservation concept may act as a useful ambassador with which to initiate such a cooperation. We have described how this might be structured within the Working in Harmony section. From this we may readily observe that, if the intent is in place, the actuality may swiftly follow. It is simply a matter of organisation. It follows logically that, if we are prepared to take this first step and establish our framework of understanding, including the establishment of practical, operational hierarchies, then we must also look towards the future and how this may be managed on an ongoing basis. Doing so uncovers some exciting opportunities for further engagement among both academia, government and the commercial world. This could easily be planned as a systematic development of the core idea and be developed in an incremental manner accordingly. Doing so would ensure that the primary initiative becomes increasingly pertinent and delivers increasing value over time. Furthermore, there are potential benefits in the area of education which might usefully be pursued.

In conclusion, this chapter has been concerned with the realities of operation from a human perspective, including management across inevitable boundaries of geography, politics and culture. Indeed many such boundaries exist, even within a single nation. The starting point for such a coordination is the realisation that we shall be working in support of the common good and that, within this model, everyone has an important part to play, no matter where they are situated. However, we have to start somewhere and individual initiatives should be ready to start using the methodology as intended. The ecological problems facing us are universal and our response should be equally coordinated and uniform in terms of its scientific foundation. Such are the objectives of the Evolutionary Conservation model.

12. Practical Collaboration

Abstract

This is a very short chapter devoted simply to one factor within the broader scenario, that of collaboration. After introducing the need for collaboration and its importance to the Evolutionary Conservation model, we shall move on to discuss some of the shortcomings with historic and contemporary collaborative efforts, including the various agendas and political baggage often associated with them. Having highlighted some of the shortcomings of current practice in this respect, we shall then introduce a new model for collaboration which fully supports the Evolutionary Conservation ethic. We describe this in detail and then move on to an exploration of what collaboration means in practice and, in particular, how our definition of a new collaboration aligns with the operational hierarchy inherent to the Evolutionary Conservation model. We shall additionally discuss the requirement for continuity and an ongoing collaboration with which to sustain and further develop our ideas and expertise into the future.

Introduction

Having made the case for a framework of understanding and the internal and external structures necessary to implement the Evolutionary Conservation model, we must now turn our attention to the practicalities of collaboration. This requirement applies at every level within the operational hierarchy, from practical field work, through intermediate administration, to the centralised management of the entire model. Individuals involved at each of these levels will require initial guidance, followed by ongoing collaborative support, both within their immediate sphere and further afield. To a degree, this collaboration will find its own level, in alignment with local and regional situations, but it may need to be orchestrated in a more deliberate manner as we move to the national and international levels.

Within this collaborative model, we might usefully define what we mean by the term 'collaboration'. At the local initiative level, this will largely be a matter of organising field research in a structured manner, ensuring that the right skills are in place, filling any gaps in knowledge as species and landscapes are identified and working together to ensure that, within the confines of the specific local initiative, every area has been adequately covered and that every species has been properly identified and understood with respect to the part it plays within the local ecosystem. Furthermore, that all seasonal variations have been identified and understood, including the presence of migratory species, and that evolutionary trends have also been captured and understood. This will often require collaboration with experts who may or may not be present locally, as well as the referencing of other sources of information. The necessary local expertise will of course develop year by year as the Evolutionary Conservation model is used in relation to specific initiatives.

The regional level has an important part to play in this context as, with a brace of local initiatives under its umbrella, trends and requirements for particular expertise may be understood and coordinated accordingly. This may include the procurement of specialist expertise which may be shared among local initiatives, as well as background information which is pertinent to all. As the Evolutionary Conservation model becomes embedded, it will itself start to provide much of this information via the feedback and feed forward mechanisms inherent in its design. At the regional level, we shall also be in a good position to spot evolutionary trends and to be able to predict future scenarios. Collaboration between all the local initiatives, together with neighbouring regional administrations will ensure that this understanding develops strongly over time.

At the national level, a very interesting picture starts to develop. The national administration will be responsible for coordinating all the regional information and ensuring that collaboration takes place among regions as necessary. This will include the sharing of expertise and specialist knowledge and may even include the provision of specialist technology where required. In this respect, the model will also prove invaluable in identifying skill shortages and suggesting areas for ongoing education and associated research. Also at this level, it will be possible to spot any gaps which become evident within the broader tapestry of understanding and ensure that steps are taken to fill them, by orchestrating the appropriate collaborative effort accordingly. The result of proper organisation at this level, in addition to passing Ecogram and Summary Statement information internationally, will be the formation of a proper annual report which succinctly captures a true picture of the national ecology, based upon informed and properly reasoned information. In most countries, this simply does not occur at present, at least not to anything like this degree. Indeed, if the Evolutionary Conservation model was followed properly, even up to this national level, it would prove extremely valuable for those nations employing it. Fortunately, it may be employed at even higher levels, from international or continental, right up to a truly global level, if a suitable administering authority may be found or otherwise put in place. At the international or continental level, collaboration takes on a subtly different meaning as it veers more towards collaboration at the administrative level, albeit with a solid scientific input in order to understand trends and potential consequences. Also at this level, there is scope to bring in subject matter specialists in key areas and to collaborate across nations in order to ensure that the best expertise is available as and where required in order to interpret the rich flow of qualified information to this level. The very fact and nature of this collaboration will ensure that valuable knowledge is shared on an hitherto unprecedented scale, all of it underpinned by field observation at the lowest level, as captured within the Ecogram and Summary Statement mechanism. The rich tapestry of understanding that such a model facilitates will surely serve us well with respect to all of our conservation initiatives, wherever they may be and whatever their particular situation. This would represent a significant step forwards with respect to conservation at the global scale and, therefore, the wellbeing of our planet.

Historic collaboration

Naturally, there has always been a degree of collaboration on initiatives of this kind. Such collaborative efforts may have been orchestrated by universities as a part of their various programmes, alternatively, there may be collaboration between commercial entities and local communities, or government agencies and others. However, in the majority of cases, these collaborative efforts would remain relatively isolated and associated with specific initiatives. In addition, we see collaborative efforts with regard to very specific situations, such as the protection of a single species, or the remediation of a specific localised situation as seems necessary at the time. Consequently, such initiatives tend to be isolated in both time and space. Furthermore, the collaborative effort which supported them would typically cease at the end of the defined programme and all the specialist knowledge developed for the occasion would be dispersed and effectively lost, excepting any documentation which, itself, will be locked in time. Collaboration of this type, while undoubtedly useful for its duration, is not terribly efficient from the longer term perspective. There is also the question of the real purpose of such collaborative undertakings. Within the academic world, the purpose will often be to secure funding in order that students can use the experience to further their own qualifications. Sometimes, when commercial entities are involved, the purpose is more aligned with public relations and political correctness. Even among government agencies, the purpose may be more aligned with perpetuating the agency itself than the broader goal of protecting our planet. It is appreciated that this sounds like a rather harsh comment on previous efforts and, of course, not all fall into this category. However, one has to be completely honest about such matters if we are to secure any tangible improvement from an ecological perspective. In addition, it is acknowledged that there exist a large number of individuals who do passionately care about conservation and have demonstrated a willingness to devote their time and expertise to the broader cause. The sort of collaborations mentioned above may often exclude such individuals if they are not students or direct employees of government or commercial organisations.

It occurs then, that historic collaborations, while achieving useful gains as far as they go, rarely take account of the broader ongoing perspective. Part of the reason for this is the parochial nature of such collaborations and their mixed objectives. One might posit that this simply reflects the human condition. However, if we are to take the longer term protection of our natural world seriously, we should strive to improve upon this situation. Future collaboration needs to be focused more upon this broader picture and be undertaken within a framework of understanding that allows the emphasis to be placed firmly upon ecological management in the global sense. This may be facilitated by a universal mechanism such as that provided by the Evolutionary Conservation model which, in itself, is aimed at supporting the common good with respect to conservation upon a global scale..

A new collaboration

What we need then, is collaboration without boundaries. A new type of collaboration whose primary objective is collaboration itself, and without any departmental or political baggage or hidden agendas. Such a collaboration will need to be orchestrated at each level by an individual or team as appropriate. At the national and regional levels, there might also usefully be a specific collaboration function which reaches out to potential collaborators and promotes the concept overall. This function may, for example, be instrumental in liaising with schools and encouraging sixth form students (and equivalents) to become involved in local conservation initiatives or, indeed, create new initiatives for themselves which may be utilised, year by year, by the school in question for successive sixth forms. Similarly with universities and, where appropriate, industrial concerns. Indeed, there are many opportunities to engage with groups of individuals or communities and inspire them towards participation in conservation initiatives.

We must also find a way for collaboration between countries in a non-political manner. This is indeed a challenge as, in many countries, the official stance on conservation is intrinsically linked with the prevailing political profile. However, there is no reason why the appropriate government agency shouldn't participate actively in the Evolutionary Conservation model while simultaneously managing its political profile. Indeed, participation in the former can only enhance the latter. Furthermore, as the concept grows and matures, participation will enable government agencies to become increasingly effective within the broader sphere of global conservation. If a given country should be the first to establish a proper framework for Evolutionary Conservation within its national boundaries, then that experience will, in a way, help to define the web of collaborations necessary to make the model work at a national level, leading to standard ways of working which may be adopted by other nations. In fact, many exciting possibilities come to mind for ways in which we may develop a voluntary framework of collaboration at various levels within the national boundary. Further afield, as we move to international or continental, there are also many ways in which we can develop practical collaborations in a workable, non-political manner. We just need to remain open minded and maintain common objectives which extend beyond the parochial. We shall also need to communicate effectively, especially in the early days when local, regional and national frameworks are being established. This communication should also include invitations to participate at various levels.

Our new collaboration is consequently a collaboration which has but one objective. To conserve our natural world at every level, in every location and to work together to this end. It is a collaboration for the common good, rather than a vehicle to serve political, commercial or personal agendas, and that is the spirit in which it should be entered into to. Sceptics will argue that such a collaboration is impossible as no one is seen to explicitly benefit or to profit from it. However, this is not the case as, in fact, all would benefit, including practitioners at every level and administrations who undertake the correlation and reporting of information. More to the point, the entire human civilisation would benefit as we shall be better able to protect and care for our natural world, both now and into the future. That is a benefit surely worth striving for.

Collaboration in practice

We have discussed collaboration at some length, but what does this collaboration amount to in a practical sense? In a word, organisation. Bringing a logical order to a wide series of initiatives and associated activities, as allowed for within the Evolutionary Conservation model. This order extends to every level within the organisational hierarchy. At the local level, it may include the organisation of human resources, including voluntary resource, and the coordination of effort from disparate groups. It may also include the procurement of tools and services as necessary to effect the planned conservational work. It will include the documentation of all activity appertaining to the local initiative including the maintenance of the annual Ecogram, as well as promotional material where applicable. This activity will merge across into the regional level where additional coordination will take place, including the sharing of expertise and associated information across initiatives. As Ecograms become embedded and built upon year by year, this information will prove invaluable at regional levels, where it may be shared at all stages.

It is at the national level where collaboration starts to become particularly interesting, both from an internal and external perspective. Looking inward, the national coordination function will be able to spot opportunities to realise economies of scale with regard to the procurement of specialist resources, tools and materials, ensuring that the best use is made of these and that results are shared and understood throughout the country concerned. This will include the ever increasing understanding of species dependencies and relationships across and within regions. From this enhanced understanding, an even richer picture of dependencies may be derived, including those at the macro level such as effects upon local climate and the early warning signs that herald such changes. Furthermore, the national administration may utilise this information in a number of ways, including reports back into national government and the preparation of information for the benefit and education of citizens. The practical activities concerned may also dovetail nicely into other areas, such as education programmes for example, or the management of development, as well as feeding into the national understanding of natural history in a particularly meaningful manner. In this respect, the Evolutionary Conservation model may be seen as a godsend for national administrations for whom the information gathered and the possibilities for how it might be used far outweigh the minuscule effort involved in managing the concept at the national level. In addition, there is a wealth of valuable public relations material inherent in such an activity which can only reflect positively on the administration concerned.

From an externally facing perspective, the Evolutionary Conservation initiative provides the opportunity for the national administration to become involved with the broader conservation effort as it feeds valuable information into the whole, for the common good of participants at the continental or global level. This will include the production of Summary Statements and reports as well as passing on Ecogram information to the higher levels within the global initiative. At each of these levels, new insights may be derived from the wealth of well informed information being passed up the chain. The national administration may take a good deal of credit from such an involvement, further enhancing the public relations appeal of such a participation. More importantly, the information that they receive back from higher levels within the hierarchy may be used to very good effect within their own national boundaries, further strengthening the effectiveness of their national, regional and local conservation efforts. The national administration may also set the operational procedures and processes for absorbing new members, maintaining the tools and information produced within its borders and generally managing the Evolutionary Conservation model from a national perspective. In doing so, it will be maintaining all necessary collaborative links and relationships, both within its own geographic boundaries and externally. All of this may be accomplished quite easily with a small team of dedicated individuals who, no doubt, already exist within a suitable government agency in the vast majority of countries.

Ongoing collaboration

Of course, having established a workable model of collaboration, such a model must itself be sustainable if it is going to realise the benefits of Evolutionary Conservation. Any such administrative functions must therefore be properly established and supported accordingly. This applies at all levels. Care should be taken therefore to establish proper operational entities, with defined roles and responsibilities in order that, even if the personnel should change, the operation may continue in a structured manner into the future. This continuity is particularly important with respect to the Evolutionary Conservation model, as much depends upon the systematic gathering of information and environmental monitoring year on year. It is this continuity over time that provides the evolutionary understanding, enabling us to better predict changes within our various habitats and ecosystems.

It is easy to understand the benefits of sustained operation over time at the local initiative level where our appreciation of the local situation becomes increasingly acute. The same is true of collaboration between operational entities. As departments and individuals collaborate and get to know one another over time, their working relationships become increasingly productive. This is true within the boundaries of a single country, between countries at a continental level and, indeed, between all concerned at a global level. As these various collaborations mature, they become increasingly effective. Coupled with the increasingly rich information provided by the Evolutionary Conservation model, this simply makes us more effective over time with respect to our conservation initiatives. It follows then that we should be looking always towards the longer term, ensuring that whatever mechanisms we put in place are both robust and sustainable into the future, including our various layers of collaboration. This, in turn, places us in a better position to manage the future of our natural world, and managing the future will become increasingly important as the human race continues to proliferate.

When a suitable central administration is established for Evolutionary Conservation, one of its functions will be to understand and document the broader collaborative model, building an international community who may work together and share the benefits provided by this initiative. Details may be published accordingly and, it is hoped, that the international community will itself grow and develop over time. An integral component of this expansion will be a robust communications programme which may also be orchestrated by the central administration. In this context, there exists a wonderful opportunity to educate as well as generally raising awareness of the need for a more extensive and better coordinated conservation effort. The Evolutionary Conservation initiative provides various tools which may be used to good effect with respect to communication at various levels.

Summary

In this chapter we have drawn attention to the need for collaboration in general, pointing out that collaboration is at the heart of the Evolutionary Conservation concept and that many of the associated benefits are only fully realised under a collaborative model. We have taken some time to discuss some of the shortcomings with respect to historic collaborations, including the politics and other agendas often surrounding them. While this situation may be understandable to a degree, it is not what we need for a broader, more collaborative conservation model, hence our drawing attention to the fact within these pages. We have further described a new model of collaboration which is much more inclusive and which holds the potential to significantly accelerate our understanding of conservation in real terms and thus better inform our various initiatives in this area. Furthermore, it has the potential to achieve this upon an unprecedented scale. In order to place this within a proper perspective, we have offered a definition of practical collaboration, explaining how this might work at every level with the Evolutionary Conservation operational hierarchy. After all, collaboration can only achieve anything when it is actually practised among participating agencies and associated groups. Lastly, we have stressed the importance of ongoing collaboration and the necessary continuity with which to ensure that the value derived from the Ecogram, Summary Statements and associated mechanisms is not only fully realised, but systematically increased over time. We should see the Evolutionary Conservation concept as a long term, continuous undertaking which will render increasing benefits with respect to conservation and the protection of our natural world. Consequently, we have devoted an entire chapter to the need for effective collaboration at every level.

13. Conclusions

Abstract

Much ground has been covered within this work and some conclusions are now offered accordingly. The importance of conservation overall is revisited and placed into a contemporary context, emphasising the possibility of previously unexperienced threats, due largely to the ever increasing human population and associated impact upon our planet. It is posited that revised attitudes and the provision of workable collaborative mechanisms will be required to mediate against these threats. The reality of complex interactions and dependencies across the natural world is emphasised, together with the need to develop a deeper understanding of the same, supported by an equal understanding of evolutionary factors, in order to better align our efforts with natural processes and ongoing developments.

Intelligent coordination and practical collaboration lie at the heart of the Evolutionary Conservation concept and the need to establish these factors in an ongoing, operational manner is discussed accordingly. This draws us into a discussion of the Evolutionary Conservation model itself and precisely why such a mechanism is required at this time. Lastly, we explore some obvious next steps as required in order to properly establish the concept and actuality of Evolutionary Conservation upon a sustainable basis.

The importance of conservation

We have understood the need for the protection of our natural world for many, many years. Ancient civilisations undoubtedly understood the necessity of working in harmony with nature and this ethic has generally been passed down over the millennia. Within the last century, scientists, authors and those concerned about our natural habitats and the species which they support have initiated a variety of projects which may come under the collective banner of conservation. Typically, these are inspired by the plight of a single species or the realisation that a habitat is being damaged as a result of human activity. Mostly, such conservation initiatives are undertaken in relative isolation, often funded in relation to a specific objective or agenda. While commendable in themselves, such projects miss an opportunity to integrate within a broader conservation effort, which might usefully take into account the complex web of interactions and dependencies which exist across both spatial and temporal domains within the natural world.

This would be a perfectly logical approach. After all, nature recognises no geographical or political boundaries, so why should we? We already understand that everything is connected upon our beautiful planet and its immediate atmosphere, and that we must understand these interactions if we are to preserve our natural environments. The necessity for developing such an understanding, and acting intelligently upon it, is more acute than ever due to the proliferation of the human race and the effect we are having upon the planet. We like to focus on such realities from both an academic and political perspective, serving a variety of agendas accordingly, but it is time we started to focus from a practical, operational perspective. It is time that the words collaboration and coordination came to mean more than simply political platitudes within high level reports. We need to find a practical model within which we can really coordinate our efforts for the common good This is the premise behind the Evolutionary Conservation initiative - to recognise the requirement for, and to provide just such a mechanism.

If we fail in our efforts to realise a better coordination and collaboration, events may overtake us and, sooner or later, we shall face the spectre of having to deal with one environmental crisis after another. Furthermore, our responses to such crises will be equally chaotic and uncoordinated, possibly fuelling even more damage to our world. The situation could quickly develop into a spiralling environmental crisis upon a global scale, escalating to the point where the civilisation that we take for granted could itself be threatened. This is not scaremongering, but simply a logical extrapolation of scientific phenomena according to what we have learned about our world to date. Looked at in this light, it is clear that we simply cannot afford to fail in this worthy endeavour. Our continued existence on this planet may be at stake.

It may be relevant to mention climate change at this juncture. Much has been written and said about climate change, often focusing upon carbon emissions as the primary agent for change in this respect. It must be acknowledged that there is a significant political context to this focus, with many agendas being served accordingly. In fact, other factors, such as habitat destruction for example (both terrestrial and aquatic) can have a very significant impact upon climate change, although this is rarely discussed. Indeed, there are a raft of associated factors, some of which may be beyond our immediate control, some of which may even be external to our planet. And, of course, it must be acknowledged that climate change is itself a perfectly natural phenomenon and would occur with or without the proliferation of human life on Earth, as it has done continually since the beginnings of our world. Nevertheless, there is little doubt that our presence and activities are having an impact upon the natural balance of the Earth's complex systems. Among these activities, continued habitat destruction and alteration (including the effect upon species) is prominent. Piecemeal conservation efforts may not be enough to stem the tide of change in this respect. We need a better coordinated, more widely deployed activity in order to take the many variables, relationships and dependencies into account and understand the broader perspective around the changes affecting our world. Some of these we may simply have to adapt to. Others we may be able to exercise a degree of control over, at least when we can see that they are detrimental to the natural common good. In any event, the concept of conservation is likely to become increasingly important as we progress through the twenty first century. Indeed, there may come a point where its importance rises almost exponentially. We should therefore be looking ahead and ensuring that we have suitable mechanisms in place with which to address this most important of issues.

Interactions and dependencies

When considering an individual conservation initiative, there is often a tendency to over-simplify the attendant issues, looking at them within a restricted context as defined by the scope of the initiative itself. Inevitably, this can lead to misunderstandings around the finer details of cause and effect. In turn, this may lead to conclusions being reached and decisions being made which, while appearing logical within the local context, may not actually be in the best longer term or wider interest. In fact, the web of interactions and dependencies which characterise the dynamics of our natural world are very complex, as we have repeatedly emphasised within these pages. Consequently, we must strive to observe, understand and document this complexity on the widest scale possible. It is only by doing so that we may develop the depth of understanding necessary to develop intelligent responses which are both sustainable and scalable. Elsewhere in this work we have described strategies which would facilitate this wider information gathering and knowledge sharing upon hitherto unprecedented scales.

There is also a dynamic element inherent in this complexity, as habitats exhibit seasonal change, species migrate, and the natural hierarchy within a given location reflects these changes. Consequently, even when focusing upon a narrowly defined locale, it may prove to have dependencies or relationships much further afield, which are not immediately obvious. In addition, there is an evolutionary context, by which this complex picture itself develops over time, according to changes within various interconnected environments and, of course, the species, habitats and ecosystems concerned. Consequently, there are many factors which may not immediately be obvious but which nevertheless may affect the wellbeing of a particular habitat from the broader conservation perspective. Furthermore, these factors may operate at a variety of scales within and external to the target conservation area. Understanding this complex web of interactions and dependencies is by no means a simple task, especially when a given conservation initiative may be small in scale and limited with respect to resources.

The answer to this conundrum lies in intelligent coordination and collaboration across a much broader scale. This, in turn, must be informed by a wide and continuous programme of observation. Wider, in fact, than anything we have attempted before. Capturing the results of such a wide observation programme, not just once, but year on year, requires a methodology and associated set of tools suited to the task. Such are provided by the Evolutionary Conservation mechanism, the use of which will systematically develop the level of understanding we seek. And, of course, this understanding, like the natural world it reflects, will itself be dynamic and subject to the same evolutionary trends. This is precisely why we must revise it, at least annually, in light of the increasingly rich intelligence provided via the Evolutionary Conservation model.

The evolutionary factor

In the previous section we have mentioned the evolutionary factor. This is pertinent as, the reality is that everything upon our beautiful planet changes, to one degree or another, over time. Even if we were able to perfectly understand a given habitat or ecosystem, together with its complex relationships and dependencies, at a snapshot in time, the likelihood is that it will change, month by month, year by year, as we progress into the future. This will be true at every scale within our target habitat. At the micro scale, organisms and species are in a constant cycle of adaptation to their immediate habitat. At larger scales, the habitats themselves are constantly adapting, responding to threats and changing conditions which, in turn, impacts upon the myriad of species supported by that habitat. It is a constantly evolving picture. Understanding this with respect to a defined area and associated conservation initiative, is complex enough. Understanding it upon a broader scale can become very complex indeed. But we must understand it if we are to be in the position of conceiving and implementing intelligent conservation programmes which are, themselves, sustainable over time. And, of course, everything that we do, intentionally or otherwise, feeds into this broader evolutionary picture.

It is important therefore, that we start to think about conservation in evolutionary terms. Our predisposition towards trying to set a given habitat into a static time window is against the tenet of the natural world and all its works. Surely, it will be better for us to understand the natural evolutionary trends and work in harmony with them, than to operate in isolation from them. In order to achieve this desirable state of affairs, we must first understand the evolutionary trends at every level, as appertaining to the habitat or ecosystem under consideration, as well as the broader evolutionary trends affecting our planet. This understanding will not come immediately but may be systematically developed over time, supported by a comprehensive programme of collaborative observation, noting changes at every level, making use of indicator species and so on. Furthermore, this understanding will itself be dynamic as it continues to be informed by reality, and will therefore require careful stewardship in order to remain pertinent and practically useful. Currently, many initiatives around the world are undertaken without any such understanding. Consequently, we have much to gain by adopting such an approach and sharing the knowledge developed without prejudice. When we have established such a model, we shall be far better placed to make informed decisions around conservation initiatives at every level and upon every scale, ensuring that all are orchestrated in sympathy with the broader evolutionary perspective. This, in turn, will place us in a much tighter harmony with the natural world, ensuring that we do not, inadvertently, trigger natural reactions which might negate all of our good intentions. This evolutionary coherence is an important and interesting factor, worthy of our best and most expert consideration. It is the nucleus of the Evolutionary Conservation idea and represents a foundation upon which a better approach to global conservation may be developed and practised. Within the Evolutionary Conservation model, simple tools have been provided that facilitate a systematic monitoring of evolutionary trends across both temporal and spatial domains. These tools may be further developed over time as we develop our own, deeper understanding of evolutionary factors in relation to conservation. We thus have a good starting point for our journey towards a better understanding of our natural world and how best to protect it in a sustainable manner.

Coordination and collaboration

Throughout this work, the importance of coordination of effort and collaboration in general has been repeatedly stressed. Actually, these are factors that the human race is not terribly good at. We like to form endless committees, associations, societies, academic departments and such like, all with attendant conferences, specific publications and various strands of activities, often undertaken in relative isolation, and we rarely coordinate them into a more general effort. The primary issue is that all such vehicles tend to be parochial and self congratulatory, very often to the point of the deliberate exclusion of others. The fact is, we are not good at sharing, although we are very good at the pretence of sharing. Of course, there is often a commercial context that quickly becomes attached to initiatives within this sphere, together with a competitive attitude among the individuals involved. Consequently, commerce and career aspirations can quickly supplant the purity of the original requirement. This observation is not intended as a criticism, merely an acknowledgement of how we tend to go about things. It is a model that, together with its political associations, has effectively acted as a check on progress in many areas. This is a great shame as, within those isolated bubbles of activity, there is some genuinely good work undertaken by individuals who are passionate about conservation. Their skills, detailed local understanding and unselfish efforts, if properly coordinated, could blossom into something much more powerful and potentially quite wonderful. We need to move to a new model. A new synthesis of ideas with a common focus, for the common good.

We don't need any more associations, political forums and such like. We already have more than we can shake a stick at and, to be truthful, they are simply not achieving the sort of effective coordination and collaboration that we so desperately need. Perhaps this is due to our tendency to create top heavy structures and political hierarchies which, inevitably, drift further and further away from the core requirements. A flatter, more laterally connected model might well suit us better and would certainly support a more practical collaboration and coordination of effort. Of course, there needs to be an administrative stewardship, but this can be maintained as a minimal, operationally efficient entity at each level. The bulk of effort and resources would be focused at the practical, operational level where they can be most effective. Fortunately, in our modern world, communication has become much easier and facilitates an active collaboration at the operational level which would have previously been much more difficult. Furthermore, the establishment of these communication links is practically realisable at relatively low cost, ensuring that information and knowledge may be readily shared. There is perhaps an irony in that it is often stated that we live in the age of communication, and yet, it is often quite difficult to communicate in a serious, interactive manner in the interests of the common good. This is not a technology issue, but a matter of ingrained attitude. Hence the need to move to a new model wherein geographic, political or cultural prejudice has no place. We can do this. It is easy. It simply requires a realignment of priorities and a realisation that there are bigger issues to consider, beyond parochial politics or individual aspirations.

Within this work, we have described an operational model which facilitates the sort of collaboration that we require in the interests of the common good. It allows for disparate teams to readily communicate and share information, building a common repository of understanding which will, in turn, illuminate and strengthen every conservation initiative under its benevolent umbrella. Furthermore, over time, this shared understanding will continue to develop as additional nodes join the network, becoming ever deeper and more relevant to our world. A world to which we all have a duty of care. It therefore makes perfect sense to collaborate and coordinate our efforts and expertise for the common good in this way. We might start small, with just a few initiatives embracing the Evolutionary Conservation model. These clusters may quickly join, developing into a larger, more vibrant entity, crossing regional and national boundaries, until a truly powerful and effective network is in place, sharing detailed information and acquired knowledge in an open manner for the benefit of all. Year by year, the depth of understanding within and across this network will increase, encompassing every habitat and ecosystem, all the primary species, every potential threat, together with examples of successful remediation. Furthermore, it will develop an overall understanding of evolutionary factors, including relationships and dependencies which could simply not be reached by individual initiatives. All of this rich information and enhanced understanding may be freely shared within the model for the benefit of all participants. In addition, all of this may be achieved with a minimum of administrative effort. Indeed, the required administration, such as it is, could easily be absorbed by existing agencies.

With such a model in place, we can maintain a shared high level vision while allowing for local variations and acknowledging the efforts and expertise across the network. Individual participants may then compare similar environments and understand the challenges faced by their counterparts in other areas. They may then collaborate as required within the network and work together to enhance specific knowledge which, in turn, will be reflected back into the broader model. This ongoing feedback mechanism will serve to systematically inform and strengthen our shared knowledge with respect to the protection and conservation of our world. From this enhanced understanding, we may develop more intelligently conceived strategies and plans for action which are in sympathy with the broader perspective. These strategies may in turn be shared and developed over time, taking into account the evolutionary understanding developed within the network. Viewed in this light, the concept of coordination and collaboration takes on a new and hugely more relevant meaning. It is all entirely realisable, if we just modify our thinking a little.

The evolutionary conservation model

One might ask why it is necessary to introduce another mechanism in support of conservation. After all, there are various existing mechanisms which have already been well considered and implemented. While it is true that there are some perfectly good existing mechanisms, these tend to have been conceived and implemented in a fairly parochial manner. Indeed, within many countries it is not unusual to find different states or regions using totally different, and non compatible, mechanisms for capturing and processing information appertaining to their various conservation strategies and initiatives. The factor which sets the Evolutionary Conservation mechanism apart is that it is universal and may be freely used by anybody. Furthermore, it has been deliberately pitched at a level which requires a minimal learning curve in order to be operational and delivering value. When used locally, it is an invaluable and potentially powerful tool. When used collaboratively across boundaries, it becomes a uniquely valuable and extensible tool. In addition, the entire Evolutionary Conservation methodology and tool set lends itself exceptionally well to educational purposes and, when used in this way, enables young students to participate in a much broader initiative, thus providing valuable experience for those wishing to pursue a career in conservation or the natural sciences generally. It may also support the teaching of evolution and the pressures upon our natural world.

However, ultimately the mechanism is what we make of it. If we embrace the idea enthusiastically, it can quickly become an extremely powerful and extensible mechanism in support of the common good. Local initiatives may continue to use elements of other systems in addition to the Evolutionary Conservation mechanism, if they perceive value in doing so (for example in support of distinct disciplines) while continuing to realise the value of the broader model. The tools and templates provided within the Evolutionary Conservation methodology are simple and intuitive in use and easily scalable from small, local initiatives to national and international conservation strategies. They consequently provide an opportunity to take global conservation to the next level. All we have to do, is use them. When we do so, we may see ways in which they can be further developed while maintaining their simplicity and universality, in which case, this may easily be achieved due to their inherent structure. The administration of any such development would need to be carefully considered and centralised in order to maintain continuity, but this is also easily achieved. Cynics may argue that we don't really need another conservation methodology, but this is a methodology with an important difference, and it is precisely this difference which empowers and supports the kind of collaborative conservation discussed within these pages. It is indeed a philosophy of conservation..

Next steps

The first step towards realising the Evolutionary Conservation aspiration has been taken with the publication of this work and the provision of the associated documentation, templates, database and other materials in support of the idea (these are available on the Evolutionary Conservation web site - see appendix 1 for details). In order to take the concept further and realise its potential, there are some logical next steps to be taken.

Perhaps the most important item in this context is communication. A simple web site has already been provided, but the real value of communication will occur when interested parties start to communicate among themselves and share ideas and experiences around using the methodology. Readers are thus encouraged to do so via whatever mechanisms they usually adopt for such purposes. The author has provided some aids in the way of slide shows and introductory documents which may be utilised for this purpose. Furthermore, in the initial stages of development, the author will be pleased to maintain a directory of interested parties accordingly. In such a manner, we may embark upon a programme of communication in order to embed the Evolutionary Conservation idea.

Assuming that the above suggestion were to meet with some degree of success then, at some stage, it will be important that a respected agency should take a lead position with regards to the ongoing centralised administration of the methodology. Initially, this may be with respect to an individual country. Ultimately, we should need an international centralised administration. This could be based almost anywhere and the author would be pleased to coordinate if a relevant agency were to step forward in this context. As with all such initiatives, there is a degree of 'chicken and egg' with regards to the proper establishment of the concept and associated mechanisms. However, we must start somewhere and the sooner we establish some sort of centralised administration, the better it will be for all concerned.

We must also consider the continued promotion of the cause and be open to any suggestions which might result in further publicity and a potential growth in the number of interested parties. If the idea gathers a proper momentum, the Evolutionary Conservation concept will be capable of delivering much information, knowledge and practical activity for the common good of civilisation. This is surely a goal worth pursuing. To date, the author has contributed a great deal of time, research and effort into developing and describing a workable model in support of this ideal. It is now time to take the next steps, to involve others, that we might, together, firmly establish the concept and methodology of Evolutionary Conservation for the benefit of all those concerned. The universality of the idea and associated mechanisms ensures that it is a methodology open to all. Furthermore, as has been suggested, there is a wonderful educational context and a potential for knowledge sharing which is simply unprecedented. Let us unite in this goal and bring something of immense value and lasting importance to our world.

Summary

This chapter commenced by establishing the ongoing need for conservation within our busy, ever expanding human civilisation. While acknowledging that the principles of conservation go back, in some respects, to ancient times, the need for a practical conservation of our natural world has never been greater, due in no small part to the burgeoning human population and the impact that this is having upon our beautiful planet. It has been further stressed that, unless we find a more efficient way of coordinating our conservation efforts, there is a real possibility that we might be overtaken by events and have to face a series of environmental crises. While such a situation might manifest itself initially in one distinct area, the impact could quickly spread and become a major issue for civilisation itself. Such a situation is easy to predict by extrapolating current situations, aligned with the impact of human growth. It is a possibility that we should be alive to and prepared for and yet, our various conservation initiatives remain largely uncoordinated.

This lack of coordination inevitably means that we have a less than ideal understanding of the complex web of interactions and dependencies, as referred to several times within this work. Projects operating in isolation necessarily have a restricted view of the world and a limited understanding of how their related actions may have a broader impact upon the natural world overall. There are many layers of this interactivity and dependency, few of which are likely to be understood or fully taken into consideration by local or regional initiatives. We must find a way of deepening our understanding and sharing the acquired knowledge upon a much broader scale. This is one of the primary tenets of the Evolutionary Conservation concept. Similarly. we must strive to understand the evolutionary factor and ensure that it is woven into our deliberations accordingly, allowing us to work in a closer alignment with natural processes. Our knowledge in all of these areas must be supported by enlightened and regular observation, undertaken upon a much broader scale and absorbed into a common understanding for the benefit of all concerned.

While speaking of coordination and collaboration, it is easy to theorise and then drop back down into familiar attitudes which, actually, are conducive to neither. We must get over this hurdle and move into a new model of true coordination and collaboration, driven by universally shared principles and a desire to act in the interests of the common good. This new wave of thinking must be underpinned by a practical model which allows this new cooperation to occur at every level, without prejudice of geography, culture, affiliation or politics. The Evolutionary Conservation initiative provides just such a model which may easily be used by anyone, and which facilitates a simple hierarchical administration with integral feed forward and feed back loops to ensure knowledge sharing upon an unprecedented scale. The requirement for such a model has been variously explored within this chapter, before progressing to consider the steps required for establishing this model in a practical manner. Moving towards a practical, operationally collaborative model is vital, not just to this idea, but for conservation in general and the well-being of our world. This reality is the nucleus of Evolutionary Conservation.

14. Appendix 1

Communication

Having read about the concept of Evolutionary Conservation, it may be that the reader would like more information about practical implementation and where to acquire the various tools discussed in this book. The primary communication channel in this respect is the associated web site. It contains much background information, together with the templates and various tools, including a database, to enable the practical implementation of the idea at all levels. In addition, there are various guidance documents and other materials with which Evolutionary Conservation may be promoted locally. There is also a Contact page where messages may be relayed back to the author. If you have found this work of interest, do please make contact accordingly. The Evolutionary Conservation web resource will be further developed over time. It may be found at http://conservation.bl.ee

Thank you for reading this book, I do hope that it has inspired you to consider afresh the concept of conservation and what it means for the future of our world.

Julian Ashbourn

September 2014

15. Appendix 2

Using Biometrics to Verify Animal Identity

A previously published paper which may be of interest to those involved in practical conservation projects.

Abstract

In this paper, a brief background into the use of biometrics for human identity verification is provided, including the acknowledgement of certain caveats which render the practice not quite as foolproof as might be supposed, while also acknowledging the benefits provided by such technologies in the general sense. The potential for using similar techniques for the identity verification of individual animals within their natural habitats is discussed, and it is posited that this might be a viable approach in support of conservation and animal welfare. The benefits of a non intrusive methodology are outlined, both for the individual and in general terms, before moving on to discuss suggestions for further research.

It is acknowledged that the idea under discussion is unusual and that, furthermore, its pursuance would present challenges beyond that faced by biometric identity verification for humans. However, such challenges might be offset by the potential for the idea across a broad range of situations in support of conservation and animal welfare. The paper is thus offered as a discussion vehicle. The author will be pleased to liaise with interested parties as appropriate in this context.

Background

Biometrics have been used to good effect with respect to human identity verification. In fact, we have been practising the principles of biometric identity verification since ancient times, albeit in a non automated manner. In more recent times, via an infatuation with measurement and what became the science of anthropometry we have variously toyed with the idea of measurement reflecting both identity and even character. With the advent of advanced machines and electronics, we further developed our ideas and throughout the past three decades in particular, the application of electronics and computer processing power to the principles of biometric identity verification has resulted in a wide range of techniques and available products and systems. In parallel, the gamut of practical applications has also developed, embracing many specialised / localised activities as well as very large scale public facing applications such as border control and law enforcement. After an uncertain start, the concept of biometric identity verification, at least for humans, has become embedded into contemporary society.

The fundamental tenet of biometric identity verification is to compare two sets of electronic data and ascertain their degree of likeness according to a preordained threshold. If the two sets of data match, we may then presume that they have the same origin (an assumption that requires qualification with the threshold level used, the granularity of the matching algorithm, the inherent quality of the samples themselves and other factors). This is the principle by which we apply biometric identity verification to practical situations.

The reader will have ascertained that there are some caveats to take into consideration and that a biometric matching transaction will, in fact, never return an absolute match due to variations in the samples employed (usually a live sample and a stored sample, although this can also entail two or more stored samples), inherent imperfections with respect to the technology employed, the precise operational conditions, user factors (where applicable) and environmental factors. Nevertheless, the technique does provide for reasonable assumptions as to likeness to be made and, importantly, introduces a degree of repeatability and, for certain applications, speed in comparing large sets of data. Matching algorithms may work on a pattern matching basis, for example measuring grey scale at pixel locations, or on a feature basis, whereby the coordinates of multiple features are plotted against a background grid and may be aligned accordingly. The analysis of waveforms, as in voice verification, is another technique and there are various other means of attempting to match instances of information captured via a biometric.

Another caveat revolves around the alignment of the biometric with demographic data as appertaining to the individuals enrolled into, or otherwise involved with the process. The accuracy of such data alignment will have many dependencies and a potential weakness exists in this area if strict controls and procedures are not employed. An example may be found with the issuance of passports incorporating biometric data. The stored biometric may or may not match the presented live sample, however, even when a strong match is obtained, there is no guarantee that the associated demographic data is correct. It may have been incorrectly entered at source or subsequently altered. We also have the issue of multiple databases to contend with, providing multiple opportunities for error as biometrics are employed and matched between them.

In view of the above observations, it will be noted that the practical application of biometric technology for human identity verification, involves an understanding of the many variables concerned and an acceptance of the inherent limitations of the combination of technology and procedure. However, the practice of biometric identity verification for humans has nonetheless become widespread and accepted as a viable identification methodology, working well in most cases. Biometric techniques include iris verification, fingerprints, facial recognition, hand geometry, vein pattern recognition, voice verification and other more peripheral techniques. These will not be discussed in depth within this paper, but information is readily available for those wishing to understand individual techniques, the detail of matching algorithms, the distinction between verification and identification, user and environmental issues and other related factors. A useful on line resource in this context may be found at http://biometrics.bl.ee

The purpose of this paper is to discuss the applicability of biometric identity verification to the monitoring of animals (or mobile organisms in general), as opposed to human beings, using similar techniques to those already developed.

Potential Application

The primary potential application might be the monitoring of animals, both individuals and groups of individuals, in the wild in order to understand their movements and their relative position as a viable ongoing species within defined habitats. This is very relevant to conservation as well as the general study of natural history and species evolution. If we can register and store non intrusive biometric data for individuals, we may find this a viable and economical way of monitoring animal movements. In addition, it would allow the development of a greater understanding of the broader picture with respect to species viability and species extinction.

It is posited that, with minor modifications to existing technology and attendant procedures, it may well be possible to adapt the principles of biometric identity verification for purposes of conservation and animal welfare. The fundamental principles of pattern matching may be used, as we do with human facial recognition for example, to recognise individuals by face, profile or other visible characteristic. Similarly, we may utilise existing voice verification techniques in order to record and subsequently recognise individual vocalisations. These are obvious applications whose efficacy may easily and quickly be evaluated in the field using relatively low cost equipment, such as imaging devices and microphones. With a little refinement, it is feasible that such techniques might be used in relation to a broad range of animals and birds at a variety of scales, possibly even insects at distinct locations or points of presence. In effect, a range of non-intrusive bio-markers might be developed, whose application could be largely automated for a variety of synergistic purposes. There are challenges to be overcome, such as relative subject scale, positioning, background conditions, incident light (for visual techniques) ambient noise levels (for audio techniques) and so on. However all of these factors and variables are well understood and may be allowed for within a given systems design.

Whether or not more specific biometrics, such as irises for example, may be relevant for certain animals is something that could be subject to further research. However, the principles of pattern matching as described would seem to be worthy of evaluation. If found to be feasible, low cost transducers could be readily deployed at strategic locations in order to capture information. Experiments could be made in the infrared spectrum or even with thermal imaging for visual operation in darkness, while the collection of audible data is of course more straightforward. Transducers could communicate via a wireless link or could store data locally for subsequent retrieval, or a combination of the two (via systematic polling for example). The resulting data could be analysed and correlated via suitable software which, in turn, could be systematically refined and developed as a result of practical field trials. In such a manner, operational systems may be readily developed and deployed within a broad variety of habitats.

Potential Benefits

There are many potential benefits to this approach. Firstly, and very importantly, such techniques may remain non intrusive and obviate the practice of animal tagging which can be costly and time consuming for the operators and distressing for the individual animals involved. Indeed, the trauma of being caught and tagged may significantly impact upon the wellbeing of individuals, with an ongoing discomfort which could cause a great deal of stress, not to mention the risk of infection. In addition, there may, in some cases, be a detrimental impact upon the local environment and even other species associated with this approach. Such a practice would seem at odds with the concept of conservation and animal welfare in general. In addition, the proposed techniques would support the use of an ever developing database of information which, unlike tags, doesn't expire and is not prone to environmental damage. Furthermore, this information may easily be shared across boundaries as required to monitor the movements of individuals and groups. This in itself brings an additional and valuable dimension to play with respect to conservation as the increasing presence or absence of species within specific habitats may be readily aligned to the monitoring of other environmental factors, as provided for via the Evolutionary Conservation model.

The equipment required for use within such a system may be kept relatively straightforward and no doubt at a low cost. Experimentation with transducers such as digital imaging devices and microphones might lead to the identification of minimal specifications for the same. Variations could exist for specialised applications as necessary (such as marine for example). From a software perspective, there are existing Software Development Kits (SDKs) which may form an experimental base, or applications may be written from the ground up to incorporate existing pattern matching knowledge. In any event, the development of such a system to the point of being usable for evaluation purposes, should not present too much difficulty.

If such a system were developed, tested and refined to a point of reliable operation within the target environment, it might be quickly deployed across other environments, realising an effective economy of scale. Furthermore, if developed along modular lines, such a system might be readily customisable for a wide range of related applications - realising further economies of scale. One could foresee the development of an almost universal system which, via simple configuration changes to a set of parameters, might be quickly deployed across a very broad range of practical applications. Indeed, the fundamental principle might be applied with a suitable scientific rigour to many situations in the natural world.

Lastly, there is a potentially wonderful opportunity for knowledge sharing and education that might be realised as a result of such a programme. Data may be normalised, correlated and shared for many related purposes and off line evaluation may be fed back to operational initiatives accordingly. There are many attendant possibilities in this context.

Recognition of Static Organisms

Another possibility occurs, that of recognising static organisms, such as flora for example within a given scene. If this were to be subject to the same principles of pattern matching and automation, then some interesting possibilities exist, especially with regard to the rarer instances of fungi, lichen and so on. Furthermore, similar techniques might serve to identify variations within species and even, perhaps to identify new species. Of course, a catalogue of sample images might become vast, but this is precisely what the power of computers and database technology can help us with. Such tools might also prove invaluable for educational purposes. Perhaps the matching techniques employed could be integrated with existing electronic 'herbals' and other sources in this context, helping, where applicable, to identify exceptions, abnormalities or even new species. This is an area which might be subject to slightly different approaches, but which might be worth considering as we move forwards.

Suggestions for Further Research

It is suggested that an organised and structured programme of research be undertaken in order to evaluate salient factors such as the feasibility of field data capture within different environments, the potential biometrics that may be used with respect to particular species, the applicability of existing matching algorithms and a plausible working methodology that might be, as far as is possible, standardised across related applications. This could be undertaken by a small consortium of interested parties if need be.

The fundamentals of straight pattern matching or the extraction and plotting of minutiae are well understood, as are the workings of image and audio transducers. Similarly, the application of matching algorithms and the distinction between the Proximity Matching Method and generalised thresholds is understood. The bulk of the work would be in applying these established principles to new operational environments and, of course, new target subjects. No doubt there will be new challenges in this context. Simple matters such as variations of pose and incident light might prove troublesome, as might the discrimination of individual vocalisations within groups. However, such challenges may be understood and overcome.

We might also usefully reconsider the requirements for associated system software and the flexibility required in order to cover a broad range of implementation. Such a flexibility may be provided by a granular user configuration section for relevant parameters. To date, most system software developed in this area has been heavily application specific (and often commercially oriented accordingly) and relatively closed to users, while it should be possible to take a more generalised approach, using open source tools wherever possible and remaining platform independent. There are many possibilities that might usefully be considered in this context. In any event, software development would likely be an iterative process and this should be reflected in the research programme plan, as should the necessity for frequent field testing and reassessment.

Conclusions and Next Steps

The next step, assuming such an idea was to be of interest, would be to identify a small group of collaborators who might move the idea forwards to the next logical position. The author has already given some thought to this area and has many ideas as to how this might usefully be accomplished. However, it is early days as yet.

In conclusion, this is something of an unorthodox idea that might initially seem very strange to those involved in biometrics for human identity verification purposes, as well as conservation practitioners. Furthermore, it is an idea whose nucleus and driving force is completely different from the world of commercial biometrics capability development. Nevertheless, it is an idea which might hold some interesting potential for those involved in conservation. With a little research and development, the viability of the idea should be quickly ascertained. If it looks promising, it might just open up an avenue of ongoing research and application which could prove beneficial across a wide range of conservation initiatives. In addition, there is some potential synergy with the concept of Evolutionary Conservation, a parallel initiative currently under development, and perhaps other initiatives. In any event, it is surely an idea worthy of further consideration.

16. Appendix 3

Grey Owl

It was the books and story of Grey Owl that inspired the author to look more closely at conservation. Here is Grey Owl's story.

Much has been written about Archie Belaney, otherwise known as Grey Owl and, of his best known companion, Getrude Bernard, otherwise known as Anahareo. Indeed, they have both documented their time together in their own best selling books. The interesting aspect, from this author's perspective, is a combination of the backgrounds which lead them to their respective paths and, in the case of Archie, the remarkable transformation in the latter years of his life, which produced that flurry of activity and documentation which so caught the imagination of the world and highlighted, not just the plight of the beaver, but the need to adopt a conservationist approach toward our remaining natural habitats. Sometimes in life, a combination of elements seem to align in space and time in order to produce something remarkable. We see this in many spheres of activity and it certainly seems to have been the case with respect to the life of Archibald Stansfeld Belaney.

One might posit that Archie's story really began with that of his father George Belaney who, by all accounts was something of a loose canon, proving to be both unreliable and somewhat irresponsible to a degree which would have been frowned upon in English society at the time. Archie's grandfather and namesake, was one of six brothers of varying character. One of the brothers, Robert became a priest and a champion of animal rights, writing prodigiously on the subject. Archie may well have come across his books in the Belaney household. Another brother, James, had the dual distinctions of becoming a physician and being tried at the Old Bailey for murdering his wife. He was acquitted but subsequently fled to France.

Archibald, Archie's grandfather, on the other hand became a prosperous merchant in London and married a well connected young lady named Julia Jackson, who had been raised by her uncle after her parents had died when she was young. Her uncle's name was George Stansfeld Furmage. Archibald and Julia had three children, George Furmage Belaney (Archie's father), Carrie and Ada (Archie's aunts). Archibald had a literary streak and composed various poems, often in a military context but, sadly, died unexpectedly at the age of forty three, when Ada was just four years old, leaving Julia to bring up the three children alone. As the sole remaining male, George was heavily spoiled by Julia who lavished every attention on him, denying him nothing and no doubt contributing to his later selfishness. George was in fact a scoundrel who, while having every advantage in life, withered away his time in pleasure seeking activities, severely depleting his mother's financial reserves in the process. One ill-considered scheme after another ended in failure and, at the age of twenty four, unbeknown to his mother, George married a fifteen year old Inn-keepers daughter who was pregnant with his child. A daughter was subsequently born, who sadly died just eighteen months later, after which George vanished from the scene. Later on, George met Elizabeth Cox and brought her home to meet his mother, and to ask for yet more financial support. His mother eventually capitulated and George and Elizabeth left for America, taking with them Elizabeth's younger sister Kittie. George bought an olive grove in Florida and, naturally, mismanaged this as he had done with every other opportunity. Elizabeth subsequently died and George married the then fifteen year old sister Kittie. It is believed that there was a daughter by Elizabeth, who was handed over to a couple in Bridgeport to look after, and George and Kittie, by now having wasted away their resources, set sail back to England. Julia Belaney met her son George and his new bride Kittie in a London hotel where George, not unexpectedly, was drunk. Julia brought them back to her new home in Hastings and a nearby terraced house was found for them while they awaited the arrival of an expected child. This time, there was at least a degree of order as Carrie and Ada took an interest in the forthcoming event, providing various assistance to Kittie. On September 18th 1888, Archibald Stansfeld Belaney made his entrance upon the world stage.

Around two years after Archie's birth, George and Kittie, who was pregnant again, decided to move away to Deal in Kent for yet another fresh start which, as usual, proved to be short-lived as George resumed his heavy drinking and ended up being temporarily hospitalised. Ada and Carrie, who by now heavily resented George for wasting away the family fortune and lacking any self-discipline, decided to act and, with Julia's blessing, rescued young Archie from what they no doubt perceived to be a fate worse than death, and brought him back to Hastings where they would undertake to give him a proper upbringing. There may exist various points of view as to whether a young child should be raised by his aunts in such a manner, but Ada and Carrie clearly had a deep affection for the child and, in any event, the alternative wouldn't bear thinking about. Goodness knows what Archie's fate may have been if he had been left under the influence of George. Kittie no doubt had all the right feelings for Archie, but was at a practical disadvantage, not being well equipped for a task such as child raising, at least not while under the influence of George. The latter continued along his wayward path until, eventually, even his doting mother realised what a disaster he had become and agreed to support him only on the condition that he left England and did not return. Kittie, who would stay, was granted an allowance to support herself and the new child who was named Hugh. An agreement was drawn up by the family solicitor and Kittie signed without hesitation. George floundered around and, from time to time, continued to bother his mother for support. It is thought that he eventually died in America following a drunken brawl. Kitty and Hugh would occasionally visit the Belaney home in Hastings and Archie would have seen his mother and brother on several occasions. Indeed, he kept in touch with Hugh for some time.

Carrie and, in particular Ada, continued to raise young Archie in an appropriate manner, determined that he would not end up like his father. It has been suggested that Ada was somewhat strict and over-bearing, yet such a view is at odds with the reality that she allowed Archie a good deal of latitude with respect to his interest in the natural world, even tolerating Archie's collection of assorted animals and insects that he would often bring in to the house. One has to place such a situation in the context of the times. This was the end of the nineteenth century and a young gentlemen was expected to be self-disciplined and properly educated. The latter requirement Ada orchestrated herself, teaching Archie a broad range of subjects and skills which would later prove invaluable to him. She tutored him at home until the age of eight, whereupon he attended a nearby Anglican church school until he was eleven years of age. The popular image of Archie's aunts as strict taskmasters and representing something to be rebelled against, is not one which this author shares. On the contrary, they appear as two loving aunts who went out of their way to care for Archie and rescue him from the influence of his worthless father. Ada undoubtedly wanted the best for him and, whether Archie understood it at the time or not, instilled in him certain principles which would eventually resurface in the Archie which we came to know. This is a familiar trend of course. Children often rebel against what they don't initially understand and then, later in life, come to know the wisdom of what was being taught to them. Just as George was a major factor, albeit unwittingly, in shaping Archie's early life, Carrie and Ada were the benevolent influence which brought stability and a sense of decency to a troubled situation. Of course, the psychological impact of not having a proper father figure would have been significant for a young lad at this time, yet he was not denied the love and affection which many children are. Indeed, Carrie and Ada may be thought of as guiding angels. They were, in many ways, Archie's salvation. Nevertheless, the Belaney streak was in the genes and Archie was no doubt incubating the restlessness and curiosity for adventure that would shape his later life. This found expression as a child in his love of the nearby woods where he would spend many hours, sometimes alone, sometimes with a friend, learning instinctively about the many creatures and how they interacted with the habitat. When Archie was eleven years of age, the family moved to a larger nearby house named Highbury Villa and Archie attended the Hastings Grammar School. His menagerie of assorted animals moved with them and Ada continued to indulge him in this activity, even though there were some worrying episodes including Archie once being bitten by an adder and requiring hospital treatment. He also suffered a couple of bouts of mild pneumonia and Ada was careful to watch over his health and general wellbeing. He did quite well in grammar school though, earning distinctions in French and English and, with some encouragement from Ada, acquiring a taste for music, expressed in his piano playing which stayed with him throughout his life, although he mixed little with the other students and was perceived as somewhat shy and withdrawn. Inside however, Archie no doubt felt quite keenly that he had somehow been abandoned by his natural parents, a feeling no doubt exacerbated by observing the other boys and their respective families. In his mind, he consequently started to invent some alternative parents, no doubt initially as a sort of wistful game, although the game was later to adopt a very real perspective. It was interesting that one of Archie's few school friends, Henry Hopkin, was also without a father at home as his parents had become divorced. Henry occasionally came home to tea and joined Archie on some of his walks but, generally, Archie liked to be alone on his forays into the woods. He would sometimes bring some of his pet animals, including snakes, into the school grounds, no doubt to impress the other boys, although it is obvious that he didn't fit particularly well with the more organised team activities at the school. The fascination with the North American Indians had already manifested itself and Archie would start to tell stories to his school chums and had even suggested that he had a touch of Red Indian blood, an assertion they no doubt found quite strange, given his background in Hastings. He had however begun to read widely on the subject and was accumulating a great deal of related knowledge, even though his perception was a somewhat romantic one at this stage. In such a manner, Archie passed his time at the Hastings Grammar School.

Upon leaving the school, Archie befriended a slightly younger lad named George McCormick who came from a well to do family who seemed to warmly accept Archie into their midst. Perhaps they were fascinated by this enigmatic young lad with an obvious love of nature and his keen passion for the North American Indian lifestyle. George, his brothers and sisters and Archie were even allowed to build a wigwam in the McCormick's garden in which the children would often sleep during the summer. Archie and George would embark on long walks into the countryside, sometimes collecting stray animals or simply observing and learning about the various species of flora and fauna to be found. Such activities were serving to shape Archie's view of the natural world, as were his encounters of less savoury activities such as fox hunting, which he always abhorred. Archie had a mischievous side to his nature which would manifest itself in many ways, including in his exploits with explosives, which he had learned about in the chemistry classes at school. He would often make little bombs and set them off in public places, delighting in the reactions they caused. An interesting facet of his inner psychology which suggests perhaps a certain rebellious streak. Archie the individual was taking shape and becoming increasingly independent. He left school and got a job as a clerk at Cheale Brothers, a local wood yard in the vicinity of St. Helen's Woods where Archie loved to roam. George McCormick would visit Archie at the wood yard and they would practice throwing knives, a skill which Archie had taught himself, as well as shooting Archie's gun. Archie's mischievous side surfaced again when he lowered some fireworks down the chimney at Cheale Brothers, which subsequently exploded in the fire below and caused much damage, an event which lead to Archie being fired unceremoniously from his position. It was clear that Archie was becoming restless and sought more adventure than sleepy

Hastings could provide, a reality which was acknowledged even by Ada and Carrie who had so wanted him to become an English gentleman. Archie had other ideas and wanted to explore further afield. Eventually, Ada agreed and, on March 29th 1906, the SS Canada sailed for Halifax with, among the second class passengers, one Archibald Stansfeld Belaney. The defining chapter in Archie's life was about to begin.

Archie's dream was to discover and live in the Canadian wilderness in a manner akin to his understanding of the North American Indians. However, he was as yet unskilled in such practices and, furthermore, would need some resources to get to where he was going, wherever that would be. Practicality dictated a stay in a thriving Toronto, where Archie got a job in a large department store selling men's wear, enabling him to start saving some money while, in the meantime reading and discovering all he could about the beautiful lands around him. When he had saved enough, Archie headed out to Lake Temiskaming, where he was met at the station by a woodsman named Bill Guppy, whose family Archie was to stay with for a while, until he had found his feet. He hoped to become a guide and Bill observed that he already had a good knowledge of animals, although he was inexperienced in trapping. He had other compensations though, in being a good story teller and being able to play on the Guppy's piano after supper, traits which endeared him somewhat to the family. Bill and his brothers taught Archie the basic skills of trapping, snowshoeing, how to handle a canoe and other things that he would need to know for a life in the wilderness. They also spoke of the Lake Temagami area, a vast forest reserve which was starting to attract tourists and Bill, his two brothers and Archie decided in the spring to make the arduous trip to Lake Temagami via a succession of canoe trips and portage across the land, another valuable learning experience for Archie. Lake Temagami is a large, beautiful lake with over a thousand islands and was home in the summer to the Bear Island Ojibwa who had been campaigning for their own reserve as they witnessed tourism taking a hold in the area, although the same developments did provide opportunities for them to become local guides. The lads from Temiskaming headed straight for the Temagami Inn where Bill and his brothers quickly landed jobs as guides. Archie however had not, as yet, the practical experience which would qualify him for such an endeavour and took instead a job as a general help at the Inn. At the end of the summer, the tourists returned home and the Guppys did likewise, leaving Archie to try and find work. In the end, he briefly returned home, sometime around the end of 1907 or start of 1908, probably to obtain some funds from his aunts, and also visited his friend George McCormick and his family. The visit seemed to instil in Archie a resolution to break with the past entirely and he was happy to return to Canada, where he started to redefine his past and develop the myth of his mixed European and Apache ancestry. He returned once again to the Temagami Inn and, in the summer, met a young Ojibwa woman named Angele, who was working as a helper in the kitchens. The two struck up a friendship, even though Angele had no English and Archie understood just a few Ojibwa words. This was a fortuitous development for Archie, as Angele introduced him to her relatives, who taught him about the Indian life style and generally befriended him. Archie met many interesting characters among the Ojibwa and learned many tales from the past, while Angele patiently taught him a basic vocabulary of the language and showed him how to set traps and fish in the lake. The Indians were impressed with Archie and his genuine desire to learn their ways, giving him the name of ko-hom-see or little owl, due to the attentive way in which he would observe all around him. He particularly struck a chord with Angele's uncle, John Egwuna and his family who, in the winter of 1909 invited Archie to come and trap with them around Austin Bay, on the south side of the lake, where they had a log cabin as a winter home. Here, Archie encountered many animals, including the beaver who were clearly quite bold and not afraid to approach the humans with whom they were familiar. He was of course in his element as this was the life he really wanted to lead and that he had dreamed of in his childhood. On August 23rd 1910, in the Fire Ranger's Hall on Bear Island, Archie married Angele.

The relationship was a good one and Angele taught Archie a great deal about the Indian ways and was clearly very fond of him. In the springtime of 1911, a baby daughter, Agnes was born. It would seem that Archie had found his ideal world. He was living the life he had dreamed about and now had a devoted wife and a beautiful new daughter. Things should have been perfect for Archie, and yet it seems that the wayward Belaney streak had not quite been erased. He spent the summer months working as a guide away from Angele and Agnes at Camp Keewaydin and then, in the autumn, stayed away and went trapping with some friends from Temagami. He returned briefly in early 1912, only to disappear again and resurface in Biscotasing, a busy little place with a Hudsons Bay Company post and a good deal of adjacent activity, including logging. Archie worked sometimes as a fire-ranger, engaged in some trapping and generally made friends in the area, where many were to remember him in later days. He was receiving regular cheques from his aunts and was generally leading a carefree life, seemingly oblivious to his responsibilities as a father and husband. Indeed, he embarked upon a relationship with a Métis woman named Marie Girard who worked as a maid at a local boarding house and, in the winter of 1913, she joined him on his trap line. The spring and early summer of 1914 saw Archie working as a fire-ranger in the Mississaga Forest Reserve, still spinning yarns about his parentage and background, developing the myth until it began to sound quite plausible, no doubt even to Archie. It was around this time that he started thinking about writing and, indeed, mentioned this to one or two of his temporary acquaintances. It was also around this time that his propensity for hitting the bottle began to be noticed. He spent the winter of 1914 once again with Marie Girard and appeared the following May in, of all places, Digby, Nova Scotia, where he promptly enlisted in the Canadian Army, declaring his marital status as unmarried. It is not certain whether Archie realised that Marie was pregnant when he left her. Perhaps he recognised the signs. In any event, a child was born, who later became known as John Jero.

There was a ruthlessness about Archie's behaviour which enabled him to simply cut himself off from those to whom he owed allegiance. In his invented background for example, he effectively denied the existence of his loving aunts who had done so much for him. Now he had cut himself off from Angele who had been equally kind to him, as well as the innocent child Agnes. Finally, after a relationship with Marie, he had left her pregnant and ran off to join the army. One might posit that these are the acts of someone who is still struggling with a feeling of rejection by his natural parents and has difficulty with close relationships. However, there are millions of orphans in the world, a great many of whom do not enjoy anything like the doting upbringing in a well to do household that Archie enjoyed. Furthermore, a great many of these less privileged children form great attachments to those who do raise them, and mature to become decent, substantial citizens in their own right. No, there was something else at work here. Perhaps it was in the form of genetic inherited behaviour, or perhaps Archie's imagination was beginning to obscure reality, or perhaps a mixture of the two. Maybe it was possible that he simply didn't see the selfishness of his behaviour, or the distress that he caused to others. He was certainly something of a loose canon at this time.

In June 1915, Archie sailed for England as an enlisted soldier in the Canadian Army. Shortly after arrival, he went absent without leave and visited his aunts, now living on the outskirts of Hastings. To the army, he had also spun a web of lies about his background and associated experience. However, he was a good shot and eventually became a sniper with the 13th Battalion of the Royal Highlanders of Canada. On April 23rd 1916 he was injured in the right foot after leaving his dugout. After examination at the military hospital in Boulogne, Archie was transferred to the King George Hospital in London, where he was to remain for four months before being transferred to Folkestone, Hastings and back to London where his fourth toe was removed at the London General Hospital. Archie was out of the war. In hospital, he struck up a relationship with one of the nurses, with whom he corresponded for some time after he returned to Canada. However, in the meantime, at his aunt's suggestion, his aunts of course knew nothing about his marriage to Angele, he had renewed his acquaintance with a childhood friend, Ivy Holmes. Ivy was an educated, well travelled young lady of twenty six years who had enjoyed being a professional dancer before the outbreak of war and, no doubt, had many interesting stories to tell which would have intrigued Archie, with his sense of the theatrical. Archie, in turn, related much of his impressions of the wilderness, its animals and associated activities, neglecting to mention that he had a wife and daughter back in Canada. Throughout the remainder of 1916 and early 1917, Ivy helped Archie to recover from his experiences of the war and they became very close. In fact, on February 10th 1917, they were married in the Church-in-the-Wood at Hollington, just outside of Hastings. Ivy was looking forward to seeing Canada and all of the beautiful places that Archie had described to her. It was arranged that Archie would return first, establish a home for them, and then send for Ivy. Archie subsequently sailed for Canada on September 19th and was never more to see poor Ivy. Once again, Archie Belaney had concocted an impossible web of lies in which he had ensnared other parties, who were to suffer accordingly. It seems almost inconceivable that he was not aware of the damage he was causing, or the cumulative nature of the complications he was constructing for himself.

Back in Canada, Archie attended hospital in Toronto as an out patient, pending his discharge from the army. He was clearly intending to return to Biscotasing and no doubt still harboured the notion that Ivy would join him there. He soon learned that Marie Girard had died and left a son, Johnny, who was being raised by a friend. No doubt confused and slightly panicky, Archie had the nerve to contact Angele, with whom he met in a small town north-east of Toronto. Angele probably knew Archie as well as anyone and was certainly aware of his true background. She knew something was wrong and was no doubt not surprised when he headed back again to Biscotasing. Young Johnny grew up until the age of ten without knowing the identity of his father, as the kindly lady, Mrs Langevin, who raised him was not exactly a fan of Archie and his erratic behaviour, not to mention his drinking habits. Archie didn't speak to the boy himself. He muddled through the next year or two, corresponding with Ivy who was still waiting to be sent for. Eventually, he let slip the truth about his previous marriage and Ivy responded in the only honourable manner, by immediately filing for divorce. In the summer of 1921, while Archie was back working as a ranger in the Mississaga Forest Reserve, the divorce papers were brought to him for signature. He apparently signed them in a nonchalant, carefree manner and carried on. This time, his aunts were of course fully aware of his behaviour and were much saddened that one of their best friend's daughters had been treated so disgracefully by the boy that they had lavished so much attention on and had, at one time, held such high hopes for. Having been made aware of Angele's existence, the kindly aunts obtained her address and sent her some dolls and a dolls house for little Agnes, then ten years of age. Archie continued with his erratic behaviour, often accentuated by a close acquaintance with the bottle, and was gaining an appropriate reputation with the locals at Biscotasing, although he no doubt enjoyed the attention that this brought. There were still those who liked him though, and would indulge him, even helping him when he went a little too far and needed sobering up.

Such was the life of Archie Belaney. He had bluffed and blundered his way along, hiding behind one mask or another and repeatedly betraying those that were dearest to him. He had a daughter and a son, both of whom he had completely neglected, not to mention poor Angele, and the hapless Ivy who had been taken in with his falsehoods. Yet, as chaotic and unreliable as Archie undoubtedly was, there was another side to him which sometimes emerged fleetingly, like a light from a partly opened door, falling upon and temporarily illuminating the darkness of his fantasy world. He had a rapport with other peoples children for example, and would occasionally bring them little gifts of oranges, sweets, or something similar. And he was beginning to feel uneasy about what he saw as the destruction of the forests for lumber and would often speak out on the subject. Perhaps Ada's tutoring and noble influence had not entirely deserted him.

A significant event in his life was meeting with Alex Espaniel, his wife Anny and their six children. The Espaniels, while ostensibly leading the life of

Ojibwa Indians, did in fact have a broader background and exposure to Europeans. Anny had worked as a housekeeper for several doctors and Alex had enjoyed a basic education and was fluent in English, French and the Ojibwa language. The Espaniels took a liking to Archie and effectively took him in for two or three years, taking him trapping at their winter trapping ground at Indian Lake before returning to Biscotasing in the spring. Alex was like a father to Archie and taught him a great deal about the Indian way of things, including a deep rooted respect for nature which helped to develop Archie's own interest in the natural world, and a badly needed sense of responsibility. Little wonder that Archie regarded Alex as a father figure. They spent long evenings talking about such matters, including tales of the old days, which Archie enthusiastically jotted down in his notebooks, an activity which had become a day to day ingredient of his life, as he was systematically building up the background knowledge which would later inform his own writings. Two of Alex's children, Jim and Jane Espaniel, forged a special friendship with Archie which endured for the rest of his life. Indeed, without the Espaniels, it is questionable whether Archie would have gained the particular understanding which later was to make him famous. They were a huge influence upon his life. However, back in Biscotasing, the Belaney wayward streak would still surface from time to time and Archie would get into trouble for drunk and disorderly behaviour of one sort or another. He was also increasingly adopting his Indian persona, learning much more of the language and even dying his hair and colouring his skin in order to appear more authentic. It was at this time that he also perfected his war dance, an activity in which he enrolled other participants, just as he had as a schoolboy when playing his Indian games. There was something of the child remaining in Archie. Always restless and seemingly at a loose end, Archie gathered his few belongings and left Biscotasing to return to Temagami in July 1925, where he acted as a guide and stayed a while with Angele who, surprisingly perhaps, still loved him. Unsurprisingly, it wasn't to last and by the autumn of that year, Archie left her again. In the spring of 1926, Angele gave birth to their second child, Flora and never saw Archie again. It was as if Archie was fluctuating between one lifestyle and another, never quite knowing which way to go. Had he stayed with Angele, at least he would not have had to maintain any pretence, as she was the one person who knew his true background, at least from a broad strokes perspective.

Such a lifestyle might have endured. However, while Archie's chaotic life was unwinding upon its particular road, there was another life unwinding which would ultimately cross his path and come to have a profound influence upon him and his future activities. On June 18th 1906 in Mattawa, Ontario a baby girl was born to a family of direct Mohawk heritage, although they had assimilated somewhat into the modern world. The child was named Gertrude Bernard and, when just four years of age, her mother died and she was raised initially by her grandmother, who told her many tales about the old days and was a major influence upon her. When her grandmother became a little too frail for the task, Gertrude was raised partly by other relatives before returning to her father, brother and sister. Her father, who was a bush worker, always maintained a keen interest and taught her many associated skills, including snowshoeing, while her grandmother taught her traditional skills such as bead work and making clothing. Gertrude, who was nicknamed Pony by her friends, loved the outdoors life and enjoyed many trips with her father among the forests. She had a lesser liking for school and, being a little headstrong, would often skip her lessons in order to go to her own little hideaway in the woods. She lived in Mattawa until, at the age of nineteen, she got herself a waitressing job at the Wabikon Resort in Temagami. Gertrude was bright and personable and impressed many guests at the resort, including two wealthy guests from America who offered to pay all the fees at a Roman Catholic boarding school in order that she might continue her education. This was to take place as soon as her summer job at Temagami ended. Fate however works in strange ways and, one day, Gertrude encountered Archie and was immediately intrigued by his appearance and apparent lifestyle which, no doubt, triggered her own sense of adventure. The two flirted together and quickly established a bond although, at this stage, Gertrude was still intending to go to the boarding school and obtain a proper education. Archie was smitten however by this bright, attractive girl who was so full of life and seemed to share his enthusiasm for the natural world. Gertrude returned home to Mattawa where, to her surprise, a knock on the door revealed Archie who had come to visit with her and her father.

Archie returned to prepare for a journey to his new trapping ground in Abitibi, northern Quebec, where he was to meet up with friends for the winter trapping season. He had been writing to Gertrude almost every day and had asked her to join him on his trap line. With his friends, he had even built a little cabin, hoping that she would come. It was by no means certain that she would accept, and no doubt Archie was very pleasantly surprised when the adventurous Gertrude decided to forsake her education and join him on the trap line. She was thinking of it initially as a temporary visit, but soon learned to love the outdoor life and was learning much from the man who she believed was an authentic half-breed Indian. In spite of the hardships, she assimilated well and stayed. After a year, Archie wrote home to his aunts, enclosing a picture of Gertrude and describing her as an Iroquois chief's daughter. He also described her, somewhat misleadingly, as his wife. Certainly, in those first few years, Gertrude got closer to Archie than perhaps anyone else had, and he revealed a good deal of his character to her, although still withheld his true identity. Due to regulations elsewhere, the trappers had flocked to Abitibi and were having a negative impact upon the lives of the Algonquin Indians who relied on the territory for their own subsistence. Archie began to understand the situation and developed an interest in Indian affairs, assisting sometimes in court cases on their behalf. He had given Gertrude the name Anahareo, which would subsequently stay with her throughout life. She admired his stance on behalf of the Indians, but started to perceive a few cracks in his character as portrayed, also noticing that his state of health was not all that it might be. Nevertheless, they continued together and, after a lovely summer in 1926, Anahareo insisted that she come out on to the winter trap line with Archie, rather than waiting alone back in the cabin. Fate was unfolding again and what was to become a momentous change was about to begin.

Anahareo, while having an affinity with the natural world was, after all, born and raised in a town environment. She didn't have the sort of ruthlessness towards animals that the trappers maintained. Consequently, she was horrified to see poor defenceless animals caught and mangled in horrific traps, some of them still struggling, only to be battered to death by Archie. She made her feelings about this known to Archie in no uncertain terms and, in so doing, sowed a seed which would develop within Archie. It all came to a head when Archie and Anahareo came across two orphaned beaver kittens. Orphaned as a result of their mother being caught in one of Archie's traps. Archie was going to shoot them, as they had no hope of surviving on their own, but Anahareo stopped him and persuaded him instead to keep the kittens. They had, after all, a responsibility towards them. Responsibility, as we have seen, was something of an alien concept to Archie. Nevertheless, he relented and the two beaver kittens quickly wound their way into the hearts of both Anahareo and Archie with their comical antics and industrious behaviour.

Fate took a hand again when Archie's mother Kittie tracked him down via the Canadian government, partly to ascertain whether she was eligible for any allowance as, following the war times had become difficult for her. Archie's brother Hugh had been institutionalised following severe shell-shock and her husband was struggling to support them. Eventually Kittie reached Archie, partly via her son Leonard who had decided to join the Hudson's Bay Company, and they corresponded. One of Archie's letters so impressed Kittie with its poetic style, that she sent it to Country Life magazine, who responded with a request that Archie should write an article for them. Archie obliged and the article was published. This was early in 1928, when Archie responded from Abitibi, and it suddenly seemed viable that Archie might write and sell articles about the wilderness that both he and Anahareo loved. It was about this time that Archie decided to stop hunting the beaver, although he would still trap for other fur-bearing animals. In the autumn of 1928, Archie and Anahareo moved to Cabano in Temiscouata where he hoped to establish a beaver colony while continuing to trap in what he had supposed was a productive area. However, the trapping was not good in Temiscouata and they soon found themselves struggling on Archie's meagre army disability pension. Archie started to write articles and sell them to Country Life, placing an increasing emphasis on himself as an authentic Indian voice from the wilderness. Unfortunately, when Archie was writing he tended to shut out everything else, including his dialogue with Anahareo who soon tired of the experience. Anahareo was equally single minded and wanted a life of her own, although she also encouraged Archie greatly in his writing. Consequently, she would, from time to time, leave Archie and go off on her own, sometimes prospecting or on other adventures. Without her steadying influence, Archie was likely to become reacquainted with the bottle, and this he did, although it didn't seem to unduly interfere with his writing. He was in fact fast becoming an alcoholic.

Fate took a hand again when, in the late summer of 1929, Archie and Anahareo journeyed to Métis, a popular resort on the St. Lawrence Estuary, hoping to generate some interest in their idea for a beaver colony. A kind Montreal lady named Madeline Peck organised a lecture where Archie presented his case, and found an unexpected supporter in the form of Colonel Wilfred Bovey, who later tried to help Archie to secure a better army pension. Others were impressed too and, in the late autumn of 1929, the Quebec City newspaper editor visited Archie and Anahareo at the disused lumber camp where they were staying at the time. The beaver man was beginning to be noticed. Anahareo went off on her own again and Archie, throughout the winter of 1929 worked hard on his first proper manuscript for Country Life, entitled The Men of the Last Frontier. But it was a mammoth task and, when Anahareo returned in the summer, he was still writing. The summer came and went, and he was still writing. In the autumn of 1930, Anahareo set off again, this time to take a job driving a dog team for tourists at an exclusive resort in the Ottawa Valley, while Archie continued with his book and also wrote several articles for the Canadian Forest and Outdoors, a publication of the Canadian Forestry Association. Impressed with the articles, the editor brought them to the attention of the Parks Branch Commissioner, James Harkin. This was fortuitous for Archie as Harkin shared his concerns for the preservation of natural habitats and had been a champion for the protection of wildlife. He immediately saw the potential and arranged for a film to be made of Archie and his beavers which he knew would provide a strong argument for conservation. In November 1930, the Canadian Forestry Association invited Archie to address their annual convention and show the new film. Anahareo left her job and came along to support Archie as he stood before the delegates. The die had been set. But Harkin saw another possibility wherein Archie could become a magnet for tourists if he were to be located in one of the national parks. Furthermore, this would provide Archie with an opportunity to both write and establish his beaver colony in a safe haven, while providing much needed publicity for the parks and their good work in the field of conservation. Early in 1931 the Parks Branch formally made its offer to Archie Grey Owl, whose fame was now spreading as a result of newspaper stories and, of course, his own writings. Archie naturally loved all the attention and gave himself the new name of Wa-sha-quon-asin, an Ojibwa word referring to the small grey, or white beaked owl, and he was subsequently established in Riding Mountain National Park in Manitoba.

The Parks Branch enlisted photographer Bill Oliver to make a new film, with which they were so impressed that they asked him to make several more. Archie got along well with Bill, whom he admired for his dedication to the job, and the short films were a great success. Later in 1931, Country Life published The Men of the Last Frontier, to considerable acclaim on both sides of the Atlantic. Archie's descriptive writing style was immediately popular with a wide audience, who lapped up his stories about the beaver and the wilderness areas. The notion that this was the authentic voice of an Indian no doubt added a little spice, exactly as Archie had intended. More importantly, Archie had embarked upon his crusade to raise awareness of the plight of Canada's natural habitats and the animals that they supported. He had in fact become a conservationist before the word was popularly understood. With this new distinction came the worry that someone might investigate his past and discover the truth about his identity and about Angele, Agnes and Flora, not to mention his other adventures. Nevertheless, Archie had the courage of his convictions and plodded on regardless. Perhaps he knew in his heart that this was likely to be a short lived episode and that he must do all he can to get his message across.

Riding Mountain National Park proved not to be ideal for the purpose and Archie was transferred to Prince Albert National Park in Saskatchewan where his beloved Beaver Lodge was established on the beautiful and peaceful shores of lake Ajawaan. It was here that Archie completed the remaining three of his four books, Pilgrims of the Wild (1934), The Adventures of Sajo and her Beaver People (1935) and Tales of an Empty Cabin (1936). By now, Anahareo was a rare feature at his side although she did spend some time at Ajawaan but, as before, could not tolerate his solitary writing marathons which left her feeling isolated and excluded. Nevertheless, the pair entertained enthusiastic visitors to Beaver Lodge which, as intended by Harkin, provided a focus for the National Parks and their potential to attract tourists. Ajawaan was not easily accessible, being well away from the main camp areas, but for those genuinely interested in nature, the journey was plausible. This was how Archie wanted it and indeed, it made sense for all concerned. Many found the experience exhilarating and were to subsequently write about it in glowing terms. Visitors included the future prime minister of Canada John Diefenbaker, who also found the experience unforgettable. By all accounts it was a great success. Meanwhile, Anahareo had become pregnant and, on August 23rd 1932, a little girl named Dawn was born in Prince Albert. While Archie loved little Dawn well enough, the child did not deter him from his writing, as Anahareo had hoped she might. Indeed, when she returned to Beaver Lodge with Dawn, they found Bill Oliver and a film crew busily at work on a new film. Another cabin had been built up on the little hill behind Beaver Lodge for Anahareo and Dawn but, of course, the familiar tensions were bound to arise when Archie was engrossed in his writing. To add to the confusion, the beavers had also taken a liking to Beaver Lodge and had built their own lodge, encouraged a little by Archie, so that it half filled the cabin which, in turn, butted on to the lake. In this way Archie could study them more closely, at least until they went away to their winter quarters. Archie's favourite beaver, the famous Jelly Roll who appeared in the films, more or less took over the lodge and had her own ideas about daily schedules. Archie liked to work at night, but Anahareo had to use the cooking facilities during the day, thus disturbing Archie when he was resting. It was a less than perfect arrangement which must have sorely tested Anahareo's patience. In the spring of 1933, she arranged for little Dawn to be looked after by a well to do English lady in Prince Albert by the name of Ettie Winters, and set off on a prospecting trip somewhere along the Churchill River. Archie wasn't much pleased with the idea, but understood that Anahareo needed a respite from Beaver Lodge. She returned later in the year but stayed at the Winter's home in Prince Albert, communicating with Archie mostly by letter.

Pilgrims of the Wild, after all Archie's hard work, was a success in Canada, America and, especially, in Britain where it was very well received, partly as a result of the promotional efforts of Archie's London publisher Lovat Dickson, an enthusiastic Canadian who had just established his own publishing house in London. It was Dickson who raised the idea of a lecture tour in Britain in support of the books. To Archie, the idea was more useful as a mechanism for raising awareness of the situation to which he had now devoted himself. Interestingly, years later, Dickson confided that Archie never even asked him about how much money the books were making. He simply wanted to reach as many people as possible with his conservation message. Lovat Dickson asked him to write a children's book and Archie set to work, delivering the manuscript in early 1935, just before the first British tour. The Adventures of Sajo and Her Beaver People was adored in Canada, America, Britain and eventually the world over, receiving a warm critical acclaim. However, the tour of Britain was to change Archie's life yet again. His lectures were so well received that they sold out almost everywhere and he made many new friends, one of whom was Mrs Betty Somervell in the Lake District who orchestrated a sell-out lecture in Kendall at the Royal Society for the Prevention of Cruelty to Animals. Archie's contingent had trouble reaching the venue and Betty went to rescue them in her new car. She invited them all to stay at her house and subsequently became their unofficial chauffeur for the remainder of the tour. Such was the impact that Archie Grey Owl was having upon the British public, who turned up in their thousands to hear him speak. But the tour was punishing, with Archie giving one, two, and sometimes three lectures a day and travelling in between times. It was a hectic schedule by any measure and the tour lasted for four months, ending in Stratford on February 8th 1936. There was a concern over who would accompany a very tired Archie back to Canada. Once again Betty Somervell stepped forward and, knowing full well Archie's tendency towards the bottle, volunteered to look after him on the trip home. It proved to be an exhausting trip for Betty who continued to look after him as they travelled through to Toronto. In Toronto, they met with, among others, Arthur Stevens, Temagami's Justice of the Peace to whom Archie had applied for a marriage license to marry Angele and to whom Ivy Holmes had written when she discovered the previous marriage. Stevens of course knew Archie's true identity, but was sympathetic to the conservationist path now being pursued by him and was content to keep the secret. Nevertheless, the encounter must have made Archie wonder how long it would be before others recognised him, and such thoughts would be an additional burden for one already living under a good deal of stress. His schedule was increasingly full with a plethora of newspaper interviews and personal appearances which were sapping his energy and there must have been moments when he longed to be back at Beaver Lodge. Betty Somervell stayed for a few days in Toronto but had, eventually, to return to Halifax and then back to England. Archie left for Ottawa and yet more meetings with prominent people. He had certainly achieved his goal of raising awareness for his conservationist crusade.

In May 1936 he was back at Beaver Lodge writing Tales of an Empty Cabin and communicating to Lovat Dickson ideas for several more books. His relationship with Anahareo had faded due to his almost fanatical approach to his writing. Ironically, as he himself noted, many of the questions he received at the end of his lectures were about Anahareo and he felt obliged to maintain the impression of their close relationship even though, in his heart, he probably knew that he had already lost her. Archie wanted to make a film about the Mississaga River area and travelled to Ottawa to meet with the Governor General and others in order to secure funding for the project. He was well received and people warmed to the idea, but decisions of this nature inevitably involve other departments and take a little time. Archie persevered, calling daily at the Department of Interior and keeping up the pressure as best he could but, in the end his resolve left him and he went out on a drinking binge. He travelled to Toronto, arriving at the station in a drunken stupor and was taken in by friends who sobered him up. He received news that little Dawn was seriously ill and rushed back to Prince Albert. Dawn recovered but Archie was really worn out and, not surprisingly, must have been close to a break-down. He had after all been overworking himself for some time now, always under the tremendous self-imposed pressure of his manufactured identity. Yet it was this very identity which was so instrumental in getting his message across, and with which he must continue if he were to achieve his objective of alerting the world to the dangers of neglecting our natural habitats. It was an unenviable position to occupy. Furthermore, while in Prince Albert, he started drinking again and ended up having a terrible row with Anahareo which seemed to seal their separation. If all this wasn't enough, the Parks Branch had been contacted by the ministry of the interior to complain about Archie's conduct, placing James Harkin in a difficult position. Harkin defended Archie Grey Owl and pointed out how successful he had been in raising publicity for the National Parks and their conservationist work, but acknowledged that, one day, they might have to reconsider the connection. However, for the time-being, Archie's job was secure. As usual, he was testing the patience and loyalty of all around him and he seemed to acknowledge how fortunate he was to maintain his position. However, his film proposal was rejected. During the summer of 1936, Archie set himself to complete Tales of an Empty Cabin. Incredibly, he had lost none of his magic and produced some of his most picturesque and poignant writing as he championed the cause of the northern forests and creatures of the wild that meant so much to him. Archie delivered the manuscript in August and the book was very well received, earning critical praise from a number of sources. In September, Betty Somervell and her husband visited Archie at Beaver Lodge and found him looking tired and weakened by the experiences of the past year. He was also visited by Lord Tweedsmuir, Governor General of Canada and others who made the journey to Lake Ajawaan. Archie spoke with Lord Tweedsmuir about the plight of the Indian and raised the idea that the Indians should become the guardians of Canada's forests and associated wildlife, being particularly well suited to the task. This idea of Indian stewardship was a theme that Archie would elaborate upon in many future discussions.

Toronto was the scene for Canada's book fair in November, to which Archie Grey Owl was naturally invited. He was scheduled to give an evening talk on November 9th at which up to 800 people were expected to attend. In the event, 1700 crowded into the room and 500 more had to be turned away. Archie had not lost his appeal to the public and, throughout the fair he gave several talks, including one to the Canadian Women's Press Club which took place in the very store in which Archie had first worked when originally arriving in Canada as a teenager. The irony was no doubt not lost on him, although his audience were oblivious of the connection. He also made numerous appearances at the fair to sign copies of his books and was a major draw. After the fair he left for Ottawa where he made contact with, among others, Yvonne Perrier, a French-Canadian whom he had met on a previous trip to the city and had taken a liking to. Yvonne was a companion and aid to Mrs Elizabeth Smith Shortt, a medical doctor at a time when most doctors in Canada were male. Archie and Yvonne had a short courtship and on November 22nd, he asked her to marry him. In early December Yvonne married one Archie McNeil at St. James United Church in Montreal. Archie now had another life's companion which he so sorely felt the need of. After some time spent in Montreal, they returned in late December to Prince Albert and arrived at Beaver Lodge on New Year's day. Time was running fast for Archie and, two months later, he set off with Yvonne to make another film, this time in the wilderness of Abitibi, with some funding assistance from Lovat Dickson and Macmillan. En route to Abitibi, Archie learned that his secret had been discovered by at least one newspaper, the North Bay Nugget. He agreed to meet with the young reporter, Mort Fellman, who was impressed by Archie and his commitment. After some deliberation, editor Ed Bunyan decided to hold the story and not reveal Archie's secret. After all, there were other momentous events occurring in the world and Archie was at least representing something positive and which had mass appeal. To destroy the myth at that stage would seem to serve little purpose.

Yvonne was a rock for Archie and provided a much needed companionship and overall steadying influence, although he was still drinking much too much. Nevertheless they completed the film and spent time in Toronto for editing purposes. In April 1937 they returned to Beaver Lodge where Archie had much work to do to prepare captions for the film which would be used in forthcoming tours. In addition, he was still intent on making the Mississaga River film which, if need be, he would fund himself and this was started in June when Archie and Yvonne set off for Biscotasing. There were two sad losses for Archie in this period. Firstly, Charlie the moose, who was so fondly mentioned in Archie's writings had been found dead and, upon reaching Biscotasing, he learned that Alex Espaniel had died the previous August. After a couple of weeks of arduous filming Archie and Yvonne headed off to Toronto to undertake the editing, and also attended an event organised annually by the Indian Defence League of America to stage a border crossing between Canada and America at Niagara Falls. They had invited Archie and Yvonne in recognition of his work to preserve natural habitats. They also found themselves much in demand to attend other functions before returning to Beaver Lodge where they busied themselves in preparation for a second British tour. In September, they set off for Montreal where they would board the Montrose liner that would take them across the choppy seas to England.

Lovat Dickson had once again organised an extensive tour, starting in London where Archie was to give fifty performances, before moving on. This time, the tour was actively managed by another Canadian hired by Dickson for the job, Ken Conibear, who got on famously with Archie and was, together with Yvonne, an enormous help. Archie worked his way through the punishing tour schedule giving superb performances which, as Ken Conibear noted, he seemed almost to make up as he went along, each being subtly different from the last. He was however in a state of near exhaustion, occasionally propping himself up with the odd drink, although this never showed in his performances. In Oxford, he met with his mother Kittie, who had approached him at the Mitre Hotel where he was staying, and they had a long chat, which, after Archie's death, Kittie remembered fondly. She also attended the evening lecture at which, in Kittie's recollection, Archie hardly took his eyes from her. They continued with the hectic tour, travelling all over the country and then, on December 10th, Archie was invited to give a Royal Command Performance at Buckingham Palace. The lecture was a great success, with much interest shown from the King and Queen and the young princesses, culminating in Archie and Yvonne being invited to stay for tea at the palace. The evening of December 14th found Archie back in Hastings where, at the White Rock Pavilion, 1400 people crammed in to hear him speak. Archie performed brilliantly and the lecture was a great success. The following morning, Ken drove Archie and Yvonne to his aunts home. Ken left to visit the sights while Yvonne and Archie spoke with Carrie and Ada, whom Yvonne believed were just friends who had put Archie up during the war. She had no idea that they really were Archie's aunts. It must have been an interesting meeting, with Yvonne being introduced as Archie's wife, when the aunts thought he was still with Anahareo, although they were, by now, no doubt resigned to expect almost anything from Archie. The kindly aunts understood the situation and refrained from reminisces of Archie's childhood. In any event, they must have been thrilled to learn of his exploits at Buckingham Palace and to see that their wayward charge had finally come good and made something of himself. Furthermore, the skills and principles that Ada had worked so hard to instil in Archie were now becoming useful, including his exposure to literature, his knowledge of the French language and his ability to deport himself as a gentleman when required. Ken returned to whisk them away all too quickly for the next step of the tour. Eventually, with the British tour completed, Archie and Yvonne sailed west to America on December 21st.

On New Years day in 1938 in New York, Archie and Yvonne parted from Ken Conibear and Archie embarked on a punishing tour of twenty eight lectures in America before returning to Canada for yet more lectures in nine different cities. Archie was achieving his dream, but at a terrible cost to his own well-being as he was becoming increasingly tired and weakened by the sheer pace and stress of such activities. By March 1938, he had given almost two hundred lectures across three countries. He and Yvonne were travelling huge distances. For his lecture on March 26th at the Massey Hall in Toronto, they had arrived just two hours before the lecture after spending seventeen hours on trains. Archie gave a magnificent two hour lecture to a packed hall of around 3000 who, in turn, gave him a standing ovation. His heart must have been overflowing. Immediately the lecture finished they were rushed back to the station where they caught the 10.50 p.m. train to Regina, the site of his final lecture on March 29th 1938.

The tour had been a magical one in many ways and Archie had brought his message of conservation directly to many thousands in Britain, America and finally Canada, while his books were reaching an even wider audience. He was exhausted and, as April dawned he really wanted to return to Beaver Lodge and rest. He finally managed to returned there on April 7th. Three days later Archie telephoned from the cabin to say that he was ill and it was immediately arranged to bring him to the Holy Family Hospital in Prince Albert where he arrived at around 11.p.m. on the Sunday night. He appeared in good spirits and seemed to be recovering on the Monday and Tuesday. Alas, at around 8 p.m. on Tuesday he developed a temperature and slipped slowly into delirium and, by midnight was in a coma. At 8.25. on the morning of April 13th, Archie Grey Owl left us for good.

Of course, the truth about Archie's identity was finally revealed, although it did little to tarnish the achievements of this remarkable man. If anything, it added to the sparkle of an extraordinary, almost fairy tale life, of one who had lived out his childhood dreams and, in so doing, had become his own creation. Much focus is brought to bear upon his deception and wayward behaviour, as well as the more theatrical aspects of his life. However, such a focus must not be allowed to obscure the fact that he was a marvellous author who brought pleasure to millions through his writing. Those who witnessed his lectures first hand were truly privileged and, for many, it was an experience that stayed with them for the rest of their lives. Most importantly, the value he brought to the conservationist cause is incalculable and remains undiminished to this day. One can hardly think about the beaver or the Canadian forests without associated thoughts of Grey Owl. Furthermore, his understanding of the Indian situation and his efforts on their behalf will be warmly remembered, ironically perhaps given his English background.

Perhaps the most remarkable thing about Archie Belaney is the transition that he was able to make between the chaotic, unreliable individual of the bulk of his life, to the highly focused, eloquent champion of nature that emerged in the last few years. It suggests that there was always, deep inside, another Archie waiting to be released if conditions allowed. The conditions would be provided by a sequence of defining events which, in retrospect, all seemed to be paving the way towards the time when Archie could finally bring everything together under the auspices of his magnificent obsession. If it hadn't been for Angele's introduction to the Indian life, or Alex Espaniel's extensive guidance, or Anahareo's enthusiastic support, or James Harkin's visionary initiative, then perhaps the necessary components would not have been in place at the right time. There is an element of benevolent serendipity in the story which seemed to unfold like the stations along a railway track, all leading to an ultimate destination, the entirety of which would be greater than the sum of the parts.

www.ingramcontent.com/pod-product-compliance
Lightning Source LLC
Chambersburg PA
CBHW081824280526
45789CB00007B/2336